Physical Characteristics

Tzu

eed standard)

SIZE
Height at withers not more than 26.7 cms (10.5 ins), type and breed characteristics of the utmost importance and on no account to be sacrificed to size alone. Weight 4.5–8.1 kgs (10–18 lbs).

BODY
Longer between the withers and root of tail than height of withers, well coupled and sturdy. Chest broad and deep, shoulders firm, back level.

COAT
Long, dense, not curly with good undercoat. Slight wave permitted. Strongly recommended that hair on head tied up.

TAIL
Heavily plumed, carried gaily well over the back. Set on high. Height approximately level with that of skull to give a balanced outline.

HINDQUARTERS
Legs short and muscular with ample bone. Straight when viewed from the rear. Thighs well rounded and muscular. Legs looking massive on account of wealth of hair.

COLOUR
All colours permissible, white blaze on forehead and white tip to tail highly desirable In parti-colours.

FEET
Rounded, firm and well padded, appearing big on account of wealth of hair.

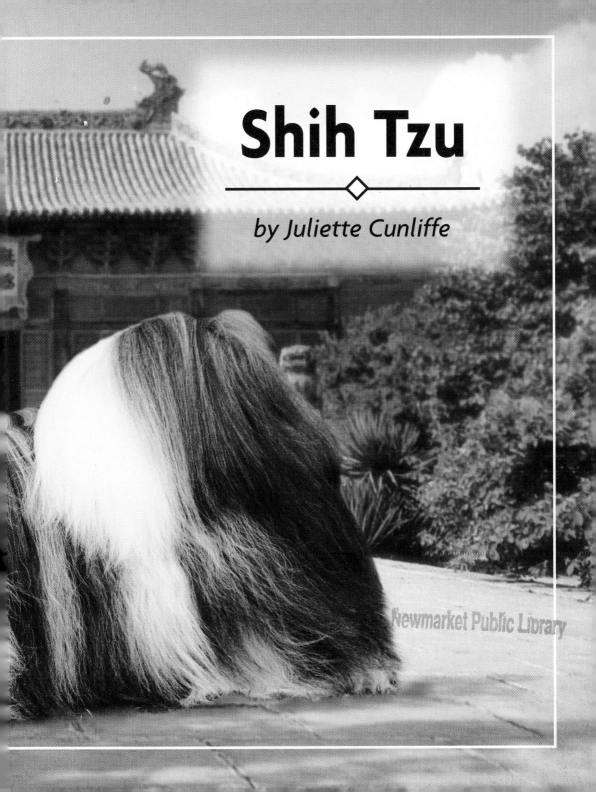

Shih Tzu

by Juliette Cunliffe

Table of Contents

9

22

History of the Shih Tzu

Examine the Shih Tzu's history as the author reveals the breed's beginnings in ancient Tibet and China; follow its evolution from the highly esteemed pet of Asian emperors to its establishment in Great Britain and beyond.

Characteristics of the Shih Tzu

Discover what makes the Shih Tzu such a unique and impressive dog: its practical size, glorious coat and confident personality all qualify the Shih Tzu as a happy and healthy pet for the right owner or family.

35

Breed Standard for the Shih Tzu

Learn the requirements of a well-bred Shih Tzu by studying the description of the breed set forth in The Kennel Club standard. Both show dogs and pets must possess key characteristics as outlined in the breed standard.

40

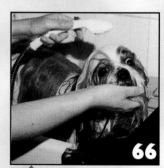

66

Your Puppy Shih Tzu

Be advised about choosing a reputable breeder and selecting a healthy, typical Shih Tzu puppy. Understand the responsibilities of ownership, including home preparation, acclimatization, the vet and prevention of common puppy problems.

DISTRIBUTED BY:

Vincent Lane, Dorking
Surrey RH4 3YX
England

Everyday Care of Your Shih Tzu

Enter into a sensible discussion of dietary and feeding considerations, exercise, grooming, travelling and identification of your dog. This chapter discusses Shih Tzu care for all stages of development.

86

Housebreaking and Training Your Shih Tzu

by Charlotte Schwartz
Be informed about the importance of training your Shih Tzu, from the basics of housebreaking, and understanding the development of a young dog, to executing obedience commands (sit, stay, down, etc.).

Photo Credits

Photos by:
Carol Ann Johnson
Additional photos provided by:
Norvia Behling
Carolina Biological Supply
Doskocil
Isabelle Francais
James Hayden-Yoav
James R Hayden, RBP

Bill Jonas
Dwight R Kuhn
Dr Dennis Kunkel
Mikki Pet Products
Phototake
Jean Claude Revy
Alice Roche
Dr Andrew Spielman
Karen Taylor
C James Webb

Illustrations by: Renée Low

137

111

Health Care of Your Shih Tzu

Discover how to select a proper veterinary surgeon and care for your dog at all stages of life. Topics include vaccination scheduling, skin problems, dealing with external and internal parasites and the medical conditions common to the breed.

144

Your Senior Shih Tzu

Recognise the signs of an ageing dog, both behavioural and medical; implement a senior-care programme with your veterinary surgeon and become comfortable with making the final decisions and arrangements for your senior Shih Tzu.

Showing Your Shih Tzu

Experience the dog show world, including different types of shows and the making up of a champion. Go beyond the conformation ring to working trials, field and agility trials, etc.

This ancient ink and colour drawing on silk
appears in a scroll executed by Chou Fang
from the T'ang Dynasty (618—907 A.D.).
The scroll depicts ladies in waiting teasing
a Shih Tzu with their insect-chasing whip.

HISTORY OF THE
Shih Tzu

The Shih Tzu is an Asian breed whose ancestry lies both in Tibet and in China. As a result, some of today's enthusiasts consider it a Tibetan breed whilst others more closely associate this adorable little dog with China.

TIBETAN BACKGROUND

Although there have been times when the Chinese and Tibetans have cooperated with each other, since the seventh century there has frequently been strife between the two nations. For the sake of diplomacy, Tibetan nobles sometimes took Chinese brides of royal rank. It therefore follows that gifts were exchanged between people of these two great cultures in which mythology abounds. Often these gifts

The history of the Shih Tzu, meaning *lion mane* in Chinese, was closely intermingled with the Tibetan-Chinese politics during the T'ang Dynasty.

were dogs. The Lhasa Apso, a Tibetan breed and direct ancestor of the Shih Tzu, is said to have existed since 800 B.C., but there is no tangible evidence of this as written historical records in Tibet were not kept until around A.D. 639.

Because the Shih Tzu descended from the Tibetan Lhasa Apso, Tibet is considered the earliest ancestral home of the Shih Tzu. Dogs were given as tribute gifts for safe passage from Tibet to China, the long journey by caravan taking eight to ten months. The Tibetan Lhasa Apsos were not considered

ANCESTRY: CHINA

Over the years, various theories have been put forward regarding the origin of the Shih Tzu. According to one theory, three temple dogs were sent to China around 1650, and from these dogs came the Shih Tzu.

sacred animals, but they were treated as prized possessions nonetheless. They were only given as gifts; never sold. The dogs were undoubtedly held in high esteem, for it was believed that they carried the souls of monks who had erred in their previous lives.

Buddhism spread from India into Tibet in the seventh century but was not adopted in China until 1253, at the time of Kublai Khan. The lion, in various mythological forms, plays an important part in Buddhism. Indeed the Buddha Manjusri, who is the god of learning, is believed to travel

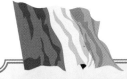

ANCESTRY: IRELAND
The Shih Tzu first arrived in Ireland with Miss Hutchins in 1928 but, until the Second World War, the breed was only known in Variety classes there. In the mid-1960s the breed grew numerically stronger, and Shih Tzu in Ireland are now fairly popular. The Irish breeders strive hard and are truly dedicated to the breed.

A young British-bred Shih Tzu shows off the desired breed type.

around as a simple priest with a small dog. This dog, called a Ha-pa, can instantly be transformed into a lion so that the Buddha can ride on its back. The snow lion, though, is considered the king of animals and it is with this white mythological beast that the Shih Tzu and Lhasa Apso are most closely connected. The snow lion is believed to be so powerful that when it roars, seven dragons fall out of the sky.

Tibetans have always drawn distinction between the 'true' lion and the 'dog' lion, but have never been too clear about the naming of their breeds. Without doubt, some crossing took place between the various Tibetan breeds. Even today it is possible to breed together two fully-coated Lhasa Apsos or Shih Tzu, and to produce one or more puppies that look like purebred Tibetan Spaniels. This may come as something of a shock, but is clearly a throwback to earlier days. Interestingly, the Tibetans refer to all long-coated dogs as 'Apsok,' which further complicates the issue when trying to research the history of Tibetan breeds.

ANCESTRY: SWITZERLAND
Although it cannot be confirmed that there were no Shih Tzu in the country before then, the first Shih Tzu registration in Switzerland was in 1956. This was the bitch Di Ji Anjou, who was imported from the Countess d'Anjou in France.

We know that the Shih Tzu can be traced back to dogs of Tibetan origin. We must also look at the dogs that were in China at that time, as these are the dogs with which the early Shih Tzu ancestors were crossed.

CHINESE BACKGROUND

The 'square dogs' that were accepted by a Chinese emperor in 1760 B.C. are believed to have been of Chow Chow type, although we do not know their size. However, in 500 B.C. there are known to have been not only dogs that followed their masters' chariots but also others with short mouths. These latter dogs were carried in the carts, so we can safely assume that they were fairly small. It has been said that the nasal bones of puppies in China were broken with chopsticks to shorten them, although the skull of an early

ANCESTRY: GREAT BRITAIN

In Britain, progeny from the Pekingese/Shih Tzu cross of the 1950s could not be registered as purebred Shih Tzu until the third filial generation. However, in the United States a further three generations were required prior to registration.

short-nosed dog housed in the British Museum has naturally short nose, the bones unbroken.

By the end of the first century A.D., emperors clearly took an interest in small dogs. A short-legged dog, known as the 'Pai' dog, belonged under the table. This may not appear especially significant until one considers that, since the people sat on the floor to eat, Chinese tables were very low. These dogs must therefore have been very small indeed. Great honours were bestowed on these small dogs; in fact, in A.D. 168 one was even awarded the highest literary rank of the period. Many male dogs were given the rank of K'ai Fu, which is just below the rank of Viceroy, whilst bitches were given ranks of the wives of such officials. These fortunate dogs had soldiers to guard them and carpets to sleep on, and they were fed only on the choicest meat.

By A.D. 1300, 'golden-coated nimble dogs' were commonly bred by people in their homes. These dogs were described as resembling the lion; indeed the Emperor of that time apparently used to love them so much that he stole them from his subjects. In China there were various small breeds of dog, including the Pug, but by 1820 the cult of the lap dog reigned supreme. Very tiny dogs, known as 'sleeve dogs,' were the height of fashion. As their name implies, these were kept in voluminous Chinese sleeves. It is still believed that their growth was stunted by artificial means; food supply was restricted and puppies were kept in wire cages until they reached maturity. Thankfully the Dowager Empress Tzu Hsi, a great lover of dogs, objected to artificial dwarfing and soon these tiny dogs fell out of fashion, finding themselves referred to instead as 'lump-headed dogs.'

THE DOWAGER EMPRESS TZU HSI

The Dowager Empress kept over a hundred Pekingese and laid down many palace rules for her dogs. Amongst these was the stipulation that they must be 'dainty in their food,' so that by their fastidiousness they might be known as Imperial Dogs. Their diets consisted of such delicacies as sharks' fins and curlews' livers, antelope milk, the juice of custard apple, rhinoceros horn and the clarified fat of sacred leopard. In an effort to stub

The Shih Tzu's worldwide popularity knows no bounds! The inspiration for artists for centuries, the breed has been preserved in every medium imaginable. Here a Scandinavian artist displays her work at a club show.

their noses, the Empress stroked and massaged the olfactory organs of her dogs, and they chewed on leather tightly stretched on a frame.

In 1908 His Holiness the Dalai Lama presented the Dowager Empress with several dogs. These were described as similar to the breed of lion dog then seen in Peking. She called these her 'Shih Tzu Kou,' and kept them apart from her Pekingese to maintain the breed characteristics of these treasured

> **DID YOU KNOW?**
> Subsequent to the introduction of the Pekingese cross in Shih Tzu breeding programmes, in 1956 a private club was set up to promote the smaller size of Shih Tzu, known as 'tinies.' Initially the Kennel Club refused permission, but permission later was granted when the club's aims had been altered.

(FACING PAGE) The Pekingese was the favourite of the Dowager Empress Tzu Hsi. She had over 100 of them in her palace at all times. In 1908 she was presented with the lion dogs that we now know as the Shih Tzu. These were a gift from the Dalai Lama and were not interbred with the Pekingese of the Empress.

gifts. However, these 'Shih Tzu Kou' did not arrive long before the death of the Empress. Although the palace eunuchs continued to breed them, it is highly likely that experimental crosses took place, thus creating a divergence in type. It is generally believed that the eunuchs bred three types of short-nosed dogs: the Pug, the Pekingese and another long-haired dog known as the Shih Tzu.

THE SHIH TZU LEAVES CHINA

Lady Brownrigg and her husband, who was later to become General Sir Douglas Brownrigg, acquired their first Shih Tzu in 1928. They had heard of 'Tibetan Lion Dogs' or 'Shock-dogs' owned by Chinese emperors, and understood that the best were to be found in Peking, where they were then living. They had seen a small black-and-white dog that rather took their fancy, and were determined to get one that was similar. The first bitch they acquired was already in whelp but, sadly, she died. However, with the help of Mme Wellington Koo, they soon found another black-and-white bitch, born in 1927. Named 'Shu-ssa,' she had a white 'apple mark' on her head and a black patch on her tail and side. The Brownriggs thought she looked like a fluffy baby owl, with her expressive eyes and hair sticking out all around her face. Her coat was thick and her tail curled over her back.

Dogs such as Shu-ssa were not often seen in public places, for they were usually kept in homes and courtyards. It was also understood that the palace eunuchs had some of these dogs, and that others had been bred by French and Russian people living in China. A Frenchman, Dr Cenier, owned a black-and-white dog of this kind and the dog, 'Hibou,' came into the possession of the Brownriggs.

Also in China at the time was Miss E M Hutchins and she, too, had acquired a dog. The dog was called Lung-fu-ssu, born in 1926. Also black-and-white, Lung-fu-ssu was heavier and coarser than those of the Brownriggs; he had a wavy coat and his tail was carried rather loosely.

In 1930 Miss Hutchins returned to England, bringing with her four dogs: the Brownriggs' Shu-ssa and Hibou, Lung-fu-ssu and a bitch called Mei Mei. Mei Mei was tragically killed by a Sealyham after coming out of quarantine. The three surviving dogs weighed between 12

Through hundreds of years of selective breeding, the Shih Tzu still maintains those physical and mental characteristics that the Chinese and Tibetans found so desirable.

(FACING PAGE) The Chow Chow breed is believed to be the square Chinese dog favoured by the emperor. Like the Shih Tzu, the Chow Chow is groomed in homage to the lion.

17

lbs 1 oz and 14 lbs 9 oz (around 5.5 kg to 6.7 kg). Although Lady Brownrigg was aware that there were other smaller dogs in China, these were not used for breeding.

THE FIRST LITTER IN BRITAIN

Shu-ssa was mated to Hibou and produced a litter in quarantine in April 1930. At that time it was possible for puppies born in quarantine to be released after eight weeks, so the puppies were carefully homed. Shu-ssa had two other litters, one later that same year, sired by Lung-fu-ssu, and another in 1932, sired again by Hibou.

By now there were several types of long-coated foreign dog in Britain. Colonel and Mrs Bailey had brought back Apsos to Britain in 1928, Colonel Bailey having taken over from Sir Charles Bell as Political Officer for Tibet in 1921. This was the beginning of a traumatic time to follow.

A club called 'The Apso and Lion Dog Club' was formed, and the first show to be held for the 'breed' was the West of England Kennel Club Show in 1933. At this show it became immediately apparent that the dogs being exhibited differed greatly, especially in length of foreface. The judge was Colonel Bailey, who made no secret of the fact that he thought the dogs imported from China were different. He expressed the belief that they had been crossed with Pekingese. What became

known as 'the battle of the noses' had begun!

Much heated argument and correspondence took place between the parties involved, and with The Kennel Club. It was suggested that the two types were differentiated by the names 'Apsos, Chinese Type' and 'Apsos, Tibetan Type,' but this did not reach fruition. Instead they agreed to The Kennel Club's suggestion of separating the dogs that had heralded from China from the Tibetan dogs. The Chinese dogs were to be re-registered as Shih Tzu.

Understandably, it was becoming impossible to judge the two breeds in the same classes at shows, but this had to be done until the separation had officially taken place. The debate continued and there was much confusion over breed names, for many owners of the dogs we now know as Shih Tzu wished to keep the word 'Tibetan' in the breed's name. They continued to refer to their breed as 'Tibetan Lion Dogs,' which did not go down well with the Apso followers. In 1934 the Tibetan Breeds Association was formed, but the Shih Tzu fraternity was not included. There was much press coverage about the heated debate concerning the two breeds, but as was said in *Our Dogs'* 'Foreign Dog Fancies' of June 22nd, 1934, '...while the Apso and Shih Tzu devotees are both standing by their guns, there is no ill-feeling on either side.'

(FACING PAGE)
A Tibetan cousin that is closer than you think! Clip away the Shih Tzu's coat and its resemblance to the Tibetan Spaniel is enlightening! As evident in the close-up, the Tibetan Spaniel's head is smaller and less round than the Shih Tzu's.

THE SECOND WORLD WAR

The problem of the difference between the breeds we now know as the Lhasa Apso and the Shih Tzu was solved, and by 1939 the number of Shih Tzu registered with the Kennel Club was 183. In 1940, instead of being registered under 'Any Other Variety,' the Shih Tzu was granted a separate register and became eligible for Challenge Certificates. However, the next major problem to occur was the Second World War, so Challenge Certificates had to wait.

Lady Brownrigg was heavily involved with work for the Red Cross. The groomings from her dogs' coats were spun into yarn, which was used to knit articles to aid the Red Cross. Breeding virtually ceased and it was a struggle to preserve the breed, which was only one of many in danger of dying out.

Following the war, a few of the original breeders resumed their showing and breeding activities. There had been a few more imports and, in an endeavour to preserve the breed, all dogs (often regardless of their quality) were used for breeding. This is the reason that some of the dogs seen at that time were far removed from the breed we know today.

THE BREED'S FIRST CHAMPION

One of the only two Shih Tzu registered with the Kennel Club during 1945 was Ta Chi of Taishan, who was to become the breed's very first champion. She descended from a Norwegian import, Choo-Choo, owned by Queen Elizabeth, now the Queen Mother. Ta Chi of Taishan's sire was Sui-Yan and her dam was Madam Ko of Taishan. The first champion was very highly regarded and even today there are those who still feel she was one of the most typical specimens of the breed.

THE SHIH TZU'S EARLY DAYS IN AMERICA

In 1936 the American Kennel Club received an application to register a Shih Tzu, and they made the erroneous statement that 'the Lhassa Terrier and Shih Tzu are one of the same breed.' Britain's Tibetan Breeds Association became involved, explaining the differences between the two. Despite several articles appearing in the American press concerning the two different breeds, Shih Tzu from the United Kingdom were exported to the United States but incorrectly registered there as Lhasa Apsos. This continued until the 1950s, and during the intervening years many of these dogs were bred from.

PEKINGESE CROSS

The history of the Shih Tzu throughout the years seems steeped in controversy. In the 1950s Miss Freda Evans, a breeder of repute within the Pekingese world and yet new to the Shih Tzu, decided that for the betterment of the latter she would introduce a Pekingese cross.

This was done without consultation with the Shih Tzu Club. One can perhaps imagine the initial reaction!

The cross was, however, correctly registered with the Kennel Club, and great care was taken in integrating the offspring into future Shih Tzu breeding programmes. Extensive breeding followed and puppies were evenly distributed up

The first Shih Tzu kennel in Germany was founded even later than those in Scandinavia, this being Mrs Erika Geusendam's Kennel von Tschomo-Lungma in 1960. In the Netherlands the leading kennel of the 1960s was that of Mrs Eta Pauptit, who had made a careful study of British and Scandinavian kennels before founding her own.

These Austrian Shih Tzu were exhibited in Slovenia.

and down the country. In time, the majority of British kennels carried some of this blood.

THE SHIH TZU IN EUROPE
In Scandinavia, Norway was the founder of Shih Tzu history, for the Danish Minister to China and his wife took the breed to Norway in 1932. The first Shih Tzu kennel in Denmark was set up in the 1940s, whilst the breed did not arrive in Sweden until 1950 and in Finland until 1955.

Shih Tzu did not arrive in what are now the Czech and Slovak Republics until 1080, but in France the story was different. The Countess d'Anjou had bred Shih Tzu in Peking long before the Chinese Revolution and had introduced the breed to France in 1950. She was responsible for writing the first standard of the breed in her country. By the 1980s the breed had become very popular in France, and is now catered for by enthusiastic clubs dedicated to a small group of similar breeds.

Shih Tzu

Apart from its incredible good looks, the Shih Tzu also has a most appealing character and is of manageable size. To keep a Shih Tzu in gloriously long coat does take a lot of work, so that is an important consideration, but a pet Shih Tzu can, of course, be kept in short coat if an owner prefers.

The Shih Tzu has become a highly popular breed, in recent years having been ranked between the eleventh and twelfth most popular breed of all in Britain. With usually well over 4,000 new Kennel Club registrations each year throughout the 1990s, the Shih Tzu is numerically the strongest breed in the Utility Group.

PHYSICAL CHARACTERISTICS

The Shih Tzu is a fairly small breed, though not as small as some, even though it finds itself exhibited in the Toy Group in some countries. Nonetheless, it is strong and sturdy for its size. In Britain the ideal height is not more than 26.7 cm (10.5 in) and the ideal weight ranges between 4.5 kg and 7.3 kg (10 to 16 lbs), although some Shih Tzu are a little heavier. Because of their sturdiness, Shih Tzu are perfectly capable of going for long walks, yet short walks suit them just fine as well; they are highly adaptable to either circumstance.

HEAD
The head of the breed has to be one of its most appealing physical attributes. Even the breed standard describes the

Shih Tzu are amongst the most popular breeds in Britain, ranking in the top dozen breeds. Surely the face of a Shih Tzu pup explains this age-old fascination with the breed.

22

The Shih Tzu's glorious coat requires much dedication from an owner. Kept in full-length show coat, the Shih Tzu must be groomed daily.

breed as having a 'chrysanthe-mum-like face,' which undoubtedly helps to give the Shih Tzu its delightful expression. Apart from the fact that the hair on the head is tied up in a top-knot, the head of the Shih Tzu is quite different from that of the Lhasa Apso and that of the Pekingese, falling as it does somewhere between the two. The Shih Tzu's foreface is not so long as that of the Apso, and the Shih Tzu's skull is broader, but compared to the Pekingese the Shih Tzu's foreface is longer and the skull is not so flat. Due to the skull shape, the eye of the Shih Tzu should be fuller than that of the Apso.

COLOURS AND COAT

A Shih Tzu in full show coat is a glorious sight, but to keep a coat in this condition certainly involves time and dedication. Not only does the Shih Tzu have a long, flowing top coat but also a substantial

DID YOU KNOW?
The Chinese historically have had some fascinating ways of describing the various attributes of the Shih Tzu. The head has been variously described as 'owl head,' 'lion head' and 'water chestnut face,' whilst the mouth has been called a 'water caltrop mouth,' 'frog mouth' and 'charcoal heater mouth.'

The art of tying the top knot. The breed's correct expression is dependent on properly tying up the haircoat on the head.

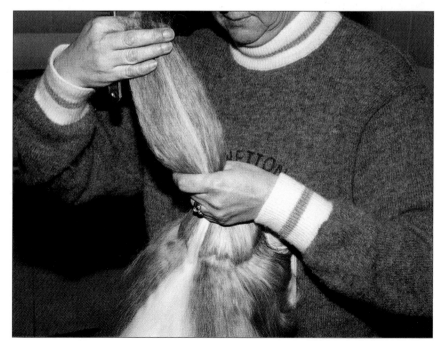

24

undercoat. This means that merely grooming the top layer may initially give a reasonably good overall appearance, but in no time at all the undercoat will start to form knots. Knots and tangles are incredibly difficult to remove if allowed to build up, so this aspect of coat care must be taken seriously into consideration before setting one's heart on the breed.

A top-knot tied correctly can enhance the features of a dog, but an incorrectly groomed top-knot can just as easily spoil the expression. Undoubtedly, doing up a Shih Tzu's head fall to best effect is an art that may take the novice months, and sometimes even years, of practice! In Britain it is usual just to have a centrally placed band in the hair, but in the United States and in some European countries colourful bows seem to be the fashion. In the USA some exhibitors even take grooming to the extreme and pad out the top-

knot with cotton wool—a vogue that is unlikely to catch on in Britain!

Many Shih Tzu pets are, however, kept in short coat, known usually as the 'pet trim.' Although this can be done at home, many owners find it easier to have the coat professionally trimmed about three times each year, although attention to the coat is, of course, also necessary between trims.

The Shih Tzu can be found in a wide variety of colours, for all are permissible. Colours range through various shades of gold to red and greys through to black. Of course, there are also parti-colours, which are predominantly white with another colour. In parti-colours a

American groomers top the Shih Tzu's head with a colourful bow, a fashion assumed by many European breeders. Thus far, the British have resisted bowing to the trend.

Black is a dominant colour in Shih Tzu.

white marking on the forehead and tail tip are highly prized. In Shih Tzu one can even find dogs that are liver in colour. These are actually permitted in the breed standard, although in this case the nose is liver in colour, rather than black, to correspond with the coat.

Because there is no colour preference in Shih

The parti-colours have gained in popularity in modern times.

really matters is the quality of the dog's construction, temperament and coat. However, if choosing a pet, colour may indeed be a deciding factor, and this is entirely understandable. After all, there is no point in buying a black Shih Tzu and, love the dog as one might, thinking for the next fourteen years or so that it was a pity you didn't have the golden colour you really preferred!

TAILS AND DEW CLAWS

The tail of the Shih Tzu should always be carried gaily, well over the back. As with the rest of the

The colour of your Shih Tzu will change over the course of the dog's life, often either deepening or fading to a degree.

Tzu, in truth an owner should not be swayed by colour. Having said that, it is only natural that some people have a purely personal preference, just as they might for the colour of their own clothing or household furniture. What

Shih Tzu, many breeders do like to have them removed when puppies are three days old. This makes nails easier to manage under the long adult coat.

PERSONALITY

The breed standard describes the Shih Tzu as being intelligent, active, alert, friendly and independent. This is indeed an

A gold and white parti-coloured Shih Tzu shows off its developing colouration.

Shih Tzu colour genetics is very complicated. Fortunately, all colours are accepted so it is largely a matter of personal preference.

dog's coat, the tail coat will need regular attention for it, too, is long and flowing. However, because of the breed's compact size, the tail is unlikely to knock your precious ornaments to the floor, as might the enthusiastic tail of a larger dog such as a Dalmatian or Labrador Retriever. A Shih Tzu's tail can indeed be an enthusiastic one, but discreetly so. It is never docked.

Although there is no stipulation as to whether or not dew claws should be removed on the

intelligent breed, though not one that demands to be constantly given new things to do as with some of the working breeds. The Shih Tzu will use his own intelligence and ingenuity to find things to do, and to watch a Shih Tzu carefully planning out what little activity to play next can be highly amusing for the onlooker—provided that

A puppy can be registered as 'bronze' and over its lifetime change to silver or gold. As unpredictable as colours are in the Shih Tzu, it's fortunate that they are mostly attractive.

the new game selected is one that will not cause any damage!

Shih Tzu are undoubtedly alert to sounds and happenings around them, but they may or may not decide to take an active part in the goings-on—that is their personality. They will decide what they want to do and, although an endearingly friendly breed, they will make up their own minds about how much or how little they choose to be involved.

This is neither a snappy nor an excessively noisy breed, though a Shih Tzu, like other dogs, will usually enjoy a good bark when the fancy takes him. Shih Tzu love to be with people. They are never happier than when with their owners, so much prefer to live as part of a family than in a kennel

THE HAIR OF THE DOG

Chinese depictions of the coat colours found in the Shih Tzu are highly descriptive and illustrative. A completely black dog was called 'Yi Ting Mo,' or 'lump of ink,' whilst one with black body and white feet was known as 'Hsueh Li Chan,' translated as 'standing in snow.' A dog with a yellow coat and white neck was called 'Chin Pi Yu Huang,' meaning 'golden cape with a white collar,' and the term 'Pien Ta Shiu Chiu,' or 'whipping the embroidered balls,' described the coat pattern of a dog with round yellow patches.

S.E.M. MICROGRAPHS BY DR. DENNIS KUNKEL, UNIVERSITY OF HAWAII

One of the fine hairs of the Shih Tzu highly enlarged.

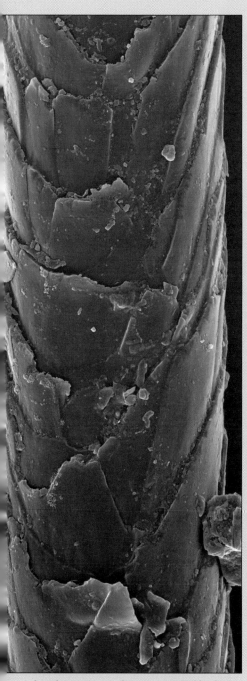

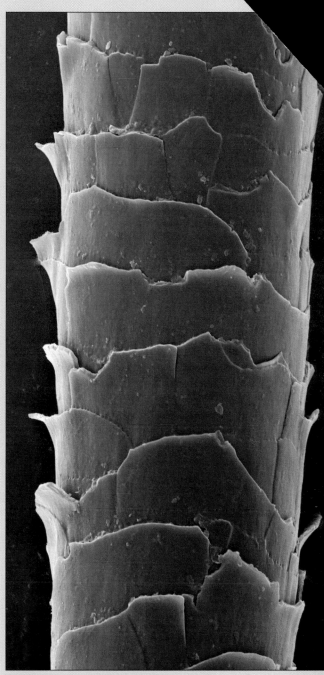

A dying hair starting to disintegrate. Hairs like this are usually brushed out in the daily grooming process.

Thick, heavy hair in perfect condition.

ituation. Although some Shih Tzu ~~o~~ take part in obedience and agility competition, they are not renowned for being a particularly obedient breed because of their somewhat independent nature.

Most Shih Tzu get on extremely well with other dogs, and often owners find they can keep several dogs, both males and females, together. Of course individual temperaments vary, so one must always introduce dogs to each other under close supervision, especially males. Although by no means aggressive by nature, males will usually stand their ground when attacked. In some cases it is therefore not a good idea to keep together males that have been used at stud, for one is sure to become the more dominant and the other

fellow may just not agree to that! Females can be rather more temperamental around the time of their season, so again caution should be exercised. In general, though, Shih Tzu are highly sociable animals in every sense of the word.

HEALTH CONSIDERATIONS
The Shih Tzu is a hardy little dog and usually a fairly healthy breed. A few suffer from veterinary and possibly hereditary problems, but this is not a breed with many major hereditary problems associated with it. There are a few common conditions, though, to which the potential owner should be alerted.

Although the majority of Shih Tzu have wide-open nostrils, a feature required by the breed

Potential Shih Tzu owners must be aware of the health problems that exist in the breed. An honourable breeder will have all dogs thoroughly checked for possible problems.

standard, tight nostrils do appear to be an inherited condition in this breed. Nostrils that are tight can be apparent at birth but sometimes cannot be noticed until between ten days and three weeks of age. However, when a puppy is old enough for sale, it should be clear whether the nostrils are affected or not.

At birth, nostrils can be so tight that they are effectively deformed and curve inwards. In other cases the nostrils are sufficiently wide at birth but tighten soon after, probably because of varying growth rate in the puppy. The nostrils usually correct themselves with time, but urgent veterinary advice should be sought nonetheless. If left to its own devices and the problem does not correct itself, such a puppy will probably grow weak and die as a result. A teaspoon of brandy added to each cup of feed has been found to help, as has keeping the puppy's environment at a constant temperature.

A condition that does not usually present a real problem, but that can frighten a new owner, is known as 'the puffs.' This is a fairly frequent occurrence in the brachycephalic (short-nosed) breeds. Because of elongation of the soft palate, a dog suddenly draws in short, sharp breaths and looks very tense, usually standing four square as he does so. This is usually brought on by the dog's

becoming very excited, but usually only lasts a matter of seconds. A quick and simple solution is to place one's fingers over the dog's nostrils, thereby causing him to breathe only through his mouth. Although this is not a major problem, it can be alarming and should always be investigated by the owner. There can be other reasons for such puffing; for

> **DID YOU KNOW?**
> China's Madam Lee considered Shih Tzu with stiff coats to be comparatively more pugnacious and aggressive than those with thick woollen undercoats, the latter generally being of a milder, gentler nature. The Chinese described the Shih Tzu's coat using images such as 'tassel-like,' like a 'waterfall' and like 'petals of garlic.'

example, a grass seed could be lodged in the dog's nasal cavity and would, of course, have to be removed at once.

Because the Shih Tzu is a reasonably long-backed breed, one should always be on the alert for possible back problems, especially in a dog's later years. In an ideal world, Shih Tzu should not be allowed to jump off furniture, although that is easier said than done! At any sign of spinal injury a vet should be contacted without delay, for in some cases even complete recovery can be achieved. Unfortunately, often partial paralysis results from spinal injury in Shih Tzu, but there are options to help affected dogs. An owner can choose to have his dog fitted with a little trolley-like device to support the dog's paralysed hind legs. Obviously, this is a serious decision to take and all of the options, however distressful, must be discussed openly with one's family and vet.

Heart disease has been noticed to occur with reasonable frequency in the Shih Tzu, and this is not just limited to older dogs. However, there are many forms of heart disease and by no means are all inherited. Obviously, any sign of such disease should be checked out thoroughly by a vet, but it should be noted that many Shih Tzu live to a ripe old age with no heart problems at all.

Because of the breed's fairly prominent eyes, it is easier for a Shih Tzu to damage his eyes than for some other breeds. An ulcer on the eye may be caused by a scratch or a knock that may have gone unnoticed. At the first sign of eye trouble a vet should be contacted because early treatment increases the chance of complete recovery. Eye problems, even those that seem small, could result in impaired vision or even loss of sight if left untreated. Reasonable care should be taken to avoid damage to the Shih Tzu's eyes, especially considering that no protection is provided when the dog's hair is tied back.

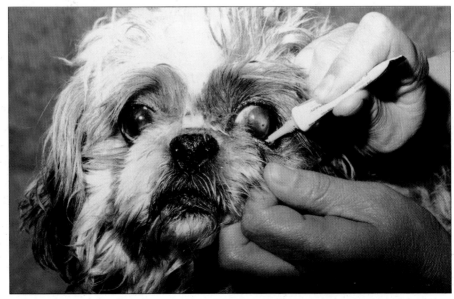

Because of the delicate nature of the Shih Tzu's large eyes, they are prone to injury. Seek veterinary assistance immediately in such circumstances.

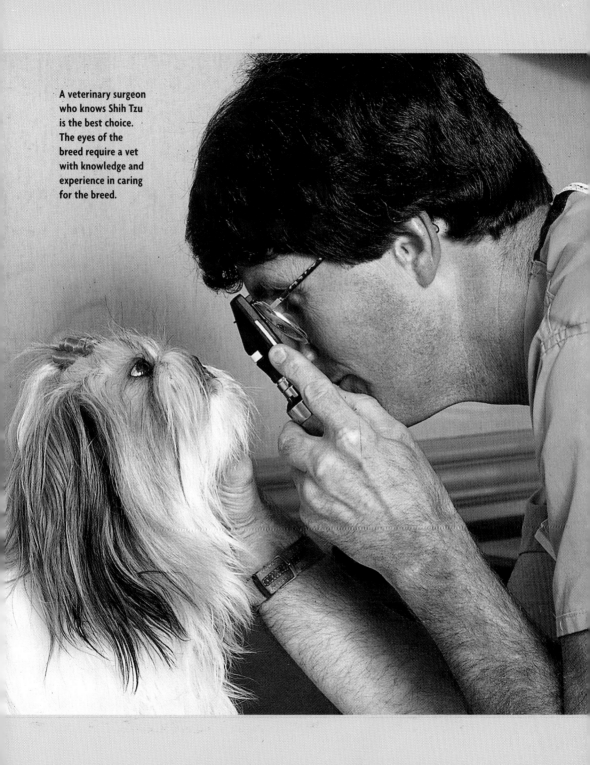

A veterinary surgeon who knows Shih Tzu is the best choice. The eyes of the breed require a vet with knowledge and experience in caring for the breed.

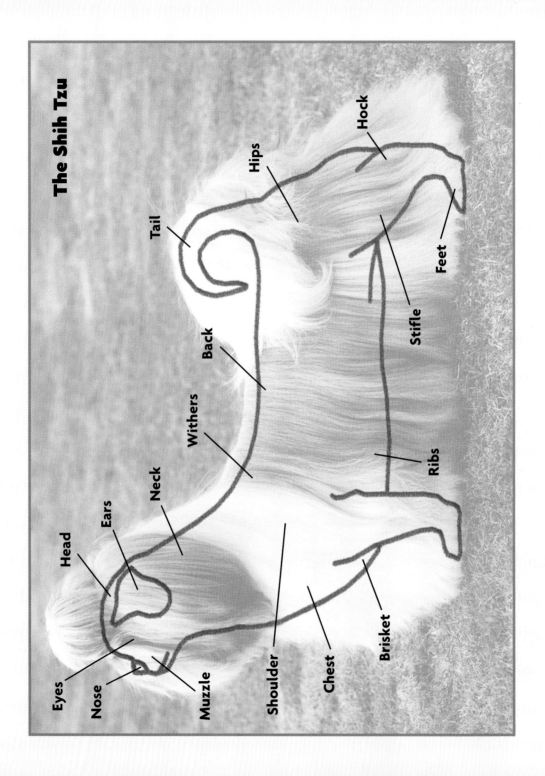

The Shih Tzu

Head
Ears
Neck
Withers
Back
Tail
Hips
Hock
Feet
Stifle
Ribs
Eyes
Nose
Muzzle
Shoulder
Chest
Brisket

Shih Tzu

The breed standard for the Shih Tzu, drawn up by The Kennel Club, is effectively a 'blueprint' for the breed. It sets down the various points of the dog in words, enabling a visual picture to be conjured up in the mind of the reader. However, this is more easily said than done. Not only do standards vary from country to country, but people's interpretations of breed standards vary also. It is this difference of interpretation which makes judges select different dogs for top honours, for their opinions differ as to which dog most closely fits the breed standard. That is not to say that a good dog does not win regularly under different judges, nor that an inferior dog may rarely even be placed at a show, at least not amongst quality competition.

The breed standard given here is that authorised by the English Kennel Club. However, in the USA the Shih Tzu is classified in the Toy Group and the overall size stipulated in the American Kennel Club's standard is rather different. Height there is 9–10.5 in (23–27 cm), but not less than 8 in (20 cm) and not more than 11 in (28 cm). Weight in the USA is from 9–16 lbs (4–7.3 kg). Whilst there are indeed differences in this regard, the English standard clarifies that 'type and breed characteristics are of the utmost importance and on no account to be sacrificed to size alone.' Something that should be common to all Shih Tzu is that the breed is surprisingly heavy for its size, so that when picked up in one's arms the weight of the dog can give one quite a surprise!

THE KENNEL CLUB STANDARD FOR THE SHIH TZU

General Appearance: Sturdy, abundantly coated dog with distinctly arrogant carriage and chrysanthemum-like face.

Characteristics: Intelligent, active and alert.

Temperament: Friendly and independent.

Head and Skull: Head broad, round, wide between eyes. Shock-headed with hair falling well over eyes. Good beard and whiskers, hair growing upwards on the nose giving a distinctly chrysanthemum-like effect. Muzzle of ample width, square, short, not wrinkled;

flat and hairy. Nose black but dark liver in liver or liver marked dogs and about one inch from tip to definite stop. Nose level or slightly tip-tilted. Top of nose leather should be on a line with or slightly below lower eyerim. Wide-open nostrils. Down-pointed nose highly undesirable, as are pinched nostrils. Pigmentation of muzzle as unbroken as possible.

Eyes: Large, dark, round, placed well apart but not prominent. Warm expression. In liver or liver-marked dogs, lighter eye colour permissible. No white of eye showing.

Ears: Large, with long leathers, carried drooping. Set slightly below crown of skull, so heavily coated they appear to blend into hair of neck.

Mouth: Wide, slightly undershot or level. Lips level.

Neck: Well proportioned, nicely arched. Sufficient length to carry head proudly.

Forequarters: Shoulders well laid back. Legs short and muscular with ample bone, as straight as possible, consistent with broad chest being well let down.

Body: Longer between withers and root of tail than height of withers, well coupled and sturdy, chest broad and deep, shoulders firm, back level.

The head should be broad and round.

Above: Long, flowing hair on head, tied up in topknot. Below: Shaved head and face to show construction of the head.

Hindquarters: Legs short and muscular with ample bone. Straight when viewed from the rear. Thighs well rounded and muscular. Legs looking massive on account of wealth of hair.

Feet: Rounded, firm and well padded, appearing big on account of wealth of hair.

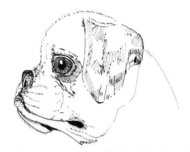

Above: Correct construction of the head and muzzle. Below: a down-pointed nose; this is highly undesirable.

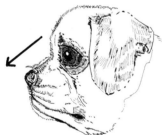

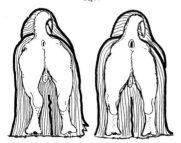

The legs to the left are cow hocks that are highly undesirable. The legs to the right are straight and correct.

Tail: Heavily plumed, carried gaily well over back. Set on high. Height approximately level with that of skull to give a balanced outline.

Gait/Movement: Arrogant, smooth-flowing, front legs reaching well forward, strong rear action and showing full pad.

Coat: Long, dense, not curly, with good undercoat. Slight wave permitted. Strongly recommended that hair on head tied up.

Colour: All colours permissible, white blaze on forehead and white tip to tail highly desirable in parti-colours.

Size: Height at withers not more than 26.7 cms (10.5 ins), type and breed characteristics of the utmost importance and on no account to be sacrificed to size alone. Weight: 4.5 to 8.1 kgs (10–18 lbs). Ideal weight 4.5 to 7.3 kgs (10–16 lbs).

Faults: Any departure from the foregoing points should be considered a fault and the seriousness with which the fault should be regarded should be in exact proportion to its degree.

Note: Male animals should have two apparently normal testicles fully descended into the scrotum.

COMMENTS ON THE STANDARD

The Shih Tzu's breed standard is fairly self-explanatory, but readers interested in showing their Shih Tzu should learn as much as possible from established breeders and exhibitors. It is sensible to attend specialist breed seminars, often hosted by breed clubs, where the finer points of the breed can be explained fully and discussed. There are, however, a few points of the standard that benefit from further elaboration here.

The nose of the Shih Tzu should be level or slightly tip-tilted. This means that when one looks at the head in profile, the nose should be roughly in line with the lower eye rim. It may be tilted slightly upward, but it is highly untypical for it to be tilted downward. The stop, which is pronounced in this breed, is the area of indentation between the eyes where the nasal bone and skull meet. Proportionately, the tip of nose to stop versus the stop to back of skull (occiput) should be 1 to 4 (or 5).

The side view of the Shih Tzu should not be square. The length is greater than the height.

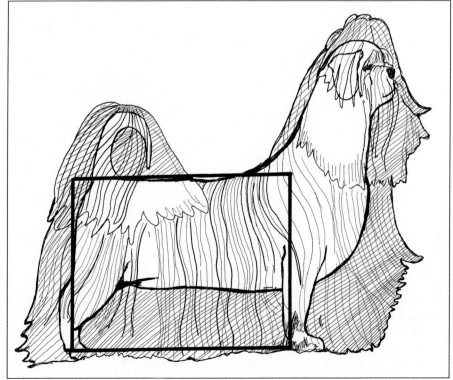

Most Shih Tzu have slightly undershot mouths, meaning that the lower incisors are positioned slightly forward of the upper ones. Although in Britain the standard allows for a level bite, meaning edge to edge, this is rarely found and is not permitted in the United States. Clearly, a scissor or overshot bite is incorrect. Missing teeth in the Shih Tzu are not heavily penalised, for in the standard the usual requirement for full dentition is not specified. However, breeders should always bear in mind that missing incisors can all too easily lead to a narrowing of the jaw, and that the Shih Tzu's muzzle should be of ample width.

There should be a clear distinction between dogs and bitches, especially evident in the head. A bitch has a distinctly feminine expression, whilst the head of the male is rather larger and more masculine in appearance.

The breed standard requires the forelegs to be 'as straight as possible.' This is because the Shih Tzu is set so low to the ground that it would be impossible to have straight forelegs whilst accommodating the depth and breadth of chest required for the breed. Having said that, in the United States the breed standard does actually call for straight legs!

The underline of the Shih Tzu is generally parallel with the line of the back, with no accentuated tuck-up, which would be untypical of the breed. When viewing the hind legs from the rear, they should be straight; the hocks should turn neither in nor out.

Movement of the Shih Tzu has been beautifully described as being like a ship in full sail. Indeed, movement displays the breed's arrogance, and the strong rear action shows the full pad of the hind feet as the dog moves away. This should be quite different from the typical movement of a Lhasa Apso, in which only a third of the pad should be seen. Provided that construction is correct, a Shih Tzu should be able to move with its head held high, without any necessity for the dog to be strung up by its lead. The high-set tail balances with the head and makes for a most attractive overall picture.

The Shih Tzu's proper gait should be arrogant, smooth-flowing, with front legs reaching well forward, strong rear action and full pad showing on the hind feet.

You have probably decided on a Shih Tzu as your choice of pet following a visit to the home of a friend or acquaintance, where you saw an adorable Shih Tzu wandering happily around the house and joining politely in the family fun. However, as a new owner, you must realise that a good deal of care, commitment and careful training goes into raising a boisterous puppy so that your pet turns into a well-behaved adult.

In deciding to take on a new puppy you will be committing yourself to around fourteen years of responsibility. No dog should be discarded after a few months, or even a few years, after the novelty has worn off. Instead, your Shih Tzu should be joining your household to spend the rest of its days with you.

Keep in mind that when you take your Shih Tzu puppy home you are making a 14-year commitment. Be certain that everyone in your household wants to live with a dog.

DID YOU KNOW?

Unfortunately, when a puppy is bought by someone who does not take into consideration the time and attention that dog ownership requires, it is the puppy who suffers when he is either abandoned or placed in a shelter by a frustrated owner. So all of the 'homework' you do in preparation for your pup's arrival will benefit you both. The more informed you are, the more you will know what to expect and the better equipped you will be to handle the ups and downs of raising a puppy. Hopefully, everyone in the household is willing to do his part in raising and caring for the pup. The anticipation of owning a dog often brings a lot of promises from excited family members: 'I will walk him every day,' 'I will feed him,' 'I will housebreak him,' etc., but these things take time and effort, and promises can easily be forgotten.

The best place to find a good Shih Tzu breeder is at a dog show where Shih Tzu are being shown. This is the ideal forum to meet breeders and make valuable contacts.

Although temperamentally a Shih Tzu is much easier to look after than many other breeds, you will still need to carry out a certain amount of training. Unlike some of the larger guarding breeds, the Shih Tzu will not respond well to overly strict training. Instead, you will need to take a firm but gentle approach in order to get the very best out of your pet.

A Shih Tzu generally likes to be clean around the house, but you will need to teach your puppy what is and is not expected. You will need to be consistent in your instructions; it is no good accepting certain behaviour one day and not the next. Not only will your puppy simply not understand, he will be utterly confused. Your Shih Tzu will

want to please you, so you will need to demonstrate clearly and consistently to your puppy what behaviour is acceptable.

Your Shih Tzu will be fairly small, and therefore probably less troublesome than a large dog, but there will undoubtedly be a period of settling in. This will be great fun, but you must be prepared for mishaps around the

DID YOU KNOW?

When breeds become very popular, and such is the case with the Shih Tzu, although there are many truly dedicated breeders, there become an increasing number of less reputable ones too. It is therefore essential to select a breeder with the very greatest of care.

41

home during the first few weeks of your life together. It will be important that your precious ornaments are kept well out of harm's (meaning the puppy's) way, and you will have to think twice about where you place hot cups of coffee or anything breakable. Accidents can and do happen, so you will need to think ahead so as to avoid them. Electric cables must be carefully concealed, and your puppy must be taught where he can go and where he cannot go.

Before making your commitment to a new puppy, do also think carefully about your future holiday plans.

DID YOU KNOW?

Your selection of a good puppy can be determined by your needs. A show potential or a good pet? It is your choice. Every puppy, however, should be of good temperament. Although show-quality puppies are bred and raised with emphasis on physical conformation, responsible breeders strive for equally good temperament. Do not buy from a breeder who concentrates solely on physical beauty at the expense of personality.

DID YOU KNOW?

You should not even think about buying a puppy that looks sick, undernourished, overly frightened or nervous. Sometimes a timid puppy will warm up to you after a 30-minute 'let's-get-acquainted' session.

Depending on the country in which you live, your dog may or may not be able to travel abroad with you. Because of quarantine laws, no dog can travel freely in and out of Britain; this must be born in mind ahead of your purchase. If you have thought things through carefully and discussed the matter thoroughly with all members of your family, hopefully you will have come to the right decision. If you decide that a Shih Tzu should join your family, this will hopefully be a happy, long-term relationship for all parties concerned.

BUYING A SHIH TZU PUPPY

Although you may be looking for a Shih Tzu as a pet dog rather than as a show dog, this does not mean that you want a dog that is in any way 'second-rate.' A caring breeder will have brought up the entire litter of puppies with the same amount of dedication, and a puppy destined for a pet home should be just as healthy as one that hopes to end up in the show ring.

Most Shih Tzu in the world are pets. You must decide on whether you want a pet dog or a show dog. Regardless, the puppy you select must be healthy and affectionate.

Because you have carefully selected this breed, you will want a Shih Tzu that is a typical specimen, both in looks and in temperament. In your endeavours to find such a puppy you will have to select the breeder with care. The Kennel Club will almost certainly be able to give you names of contacts within Shih Tzu breed clubs. These people can possibly put you in touch with breeders who may have puppies for sale. However, although they can point you in the right direction, it will be up to you to do your homework carefully.

Even though you are probably not looking for a show dog, it is always a good idea to visit a show so that you can see quality specimens of the breed. This will also give you an opportunity to

meet breeders who will probably be able to answer some of your queries. In addition, you will get some idea about which breeders appear to take most care of their stock and which are likely to have given their puppies the best possible start in life. Something else you may be able to decide

DID YOU KNOW?

Your puppy should have a well-fed appearance but not a distended abdomen, which may indicate worms or incorrect feeding, or both. The body should be firm, with a solid feel. The skin of the abdomen should be pale pink and clean, without signs of scratching or rash. Check the hind legs to make certain that dewclaws were removed, if any were present at birth.

43

upon is which colour appeals to you most, although this is purely personal preference.

When buying your puppy, you will need to know about vaccinations: which ones have been given already and which ones the puppy still needs. It is important that any injections already given by a veterinary surgeon have been

DOCUMENTATION

Two important documents you will get from the breeder are the pup's pedigree and registration papers. The breeder should register the litter and each pup with The Kennel Club, and it is necessary for you to have the paperwork if you plan on showing or breeding in the future.

Make sure you know the breeder's intentions on which type of registration he will obtain for the pup. There are limited registrations which may prohibit the dog from being shown or from competing in non-conformation trials such as Working or Agility if the breeder feels that the pup is not of sufficient quality to do so. There is also a type of registration that will permit the dog in non-conformation competition only.

If your dog is registered with a Kennel-Club-recognised breed club, then you can register the pup with The Kennel Club yourself. Your breeder can assist you with the specifics of the registration process.

DID YOU KNOW?

Breeders rarely release puppies until they are eight to ten weeks of age. This is an acceptable age for most breeds of dog, excepting toy breeds which are not released until around 12 weeks, given their petite sizes. If a breeder has a puppy that is 12 weeks or more, it is likely well socialised and housetrained. Be sure that it is otherwise healthy before deciding to take it home.

recorded and documented for proof. A worming routine is also vital for any young puppy, so the breeder should be able to tell you exactly what treatment has been given, when it was administered and how you should continue.

Clearly, when selecting a puppy, the one you choose must be in good condition. The coat should look healthy and there should be no discharge from the eyes or nose. Ears should also be clean and, of course, there should be absolutely no sign of parasites. Check that the skin is healthy and free of rashes and irritations. Of course, the puppy you choose should not have any evidence of loose stool.

As in several other breeds, some Shih Tzu puppies have

A ten-day-old Shih Tzu puppy with its eyes just opened. Puppies should be about 12 weeks old before they are removed from the dam.

You can visit a breeder and choose your puppy even before it is ready to leave its mother. Ideally you will be able to meet the dam of your puppy to get a firm idea of the temperament and other attributes.

INSURANCE

Many good breeders will offer you insurance with your new puppy, which is an excellent idea. The first few weeks of insurance will probably be covered free of charge or with only minimal cost, allowing you to take up the policy when this expires. If you own a pet dog, it is sensible to take out such a policy as veterinary fees can be high, although routine vaccinations and boosters are not covered. Look carefully at the many options open to you before deciding which suits best.

ARE YOU A FIT OWNER?

If the breeder from whom you are buying a puppy asks you a lot of personal questions, do not be insulted. Such a breeder wants to be sure that you will be a fit provider for his puppy.

umbilical hernias, which can be seen as a small lump on the tummy where the umbilical cord was attached. It is preferable not to have such a hernia on any puppy, but you should check for this at the outset. If a hernia is present, you should discuss its seriousness with the breeder. Most umbilical hernias are safe, but your vet should keep an eye on it in case an operation is needed.

A newly born Shih Tzu puppy only 24 hours old. Its eyes are still closed.

Just a few words of warning: Be very careful about where you purchase your puppy. Find your breeder through a reputable source, like a breed club, and visit the quarters in which the pups are kept. Always insist that you see the puppy's dam and, if possible, the sire. While frequently the sire will not be owned by the litter's breeder, a photograph may be available for you to see. Ask if the breeder

has any other of the puppy's relatives that you can meet. For example, there may be an older half-sister or half-brother, and it would be interesting for you to see how they have turned out: their eventual size, coat quality, temperament and so on.

Be sure, too, that if you decide to buy a puppy, all relevant documentation is provided at the time of sale. You will need a copy of the pedigree, preferably Kennel Club registration documents, vaccination certificates and a feeding chart so that you know exactly how

the puppy has been fed and how you should continue. Some careful breeders provide their puppy buyers with a small amount of food. This prevents the risk of an upset tummy, allowing for a gradual change of diet if that particular brand of food is not locally available.

Spend as much time observing the puppies as possible. Often the juvenile personality gives a preview of an adult temperament. The consideration of the puppy's sex should be decided before you visit the litter.

COMMITMENT OF OWNERSHIP

After considering all of these factors, you have already made some very important decisions about selecting your puppy. You have chosen a Shih Tzu, which means that you have decided which characteristics you want in a dog and what type of dog will best fit into your family and lifestyle. If you have selected a breeder, you have gone a step further—you have done your research and found a responsible, conscientious person who breeds quality Shih Tzu and who should be a reliable source of help as you and your puppy adjust to life together. If you have observed a litter in action, you have obtained a firsthand look at the dynamics of a puppy 'pack' and, thus, you should learn about each pup's individual personality—perhaps you have even found one that particularly appeals to you.

However, even if you have not yet found the Shih Tzu puppy of

YOUR SCHEDULE...

If you lead an erratic, unpredictable life, with daily or weekly changes in your work requirements, consider the problems of owning a puppy. The new puppy has to be fed regularly, socialised (loved, petted, handled, introduced to other people) and, most importantly, allowed to visit outdoors for toilet training. As the dog gets older, it can be more tolerant of deviations in its feeding and toilet relief.

your dreams, observing pups will help you learn to recognise certain behaviour and to determine what a pup's behaviour indicates about his temperament. You will be able to pick out which pups are the leaders, which ones are less outgoing, which ones are confident, which ones are shy, playful, friendly, aggressive, etc. Equally as important, you will learn to recognise what a healthy pup should look and act like. All of these things will help you in your search, and when you find the Shih Tzu that was meant for you, you will know it!

Researching your breed, selecting a responsible breeder and observing as many pups as possible are all important steps on the way to dog ownership. It may seem like a lot of effort...and you have not even brought the pup home yet! Remember, though, you cannot be too careful

DID YOU KNOW?

The cost of food must also be mentioned. All dogs need a good quality food with an adequate supply of protein to develop their bones and muscles properly. Most dogs are not picky eaters but unless fed properly they can quickly succumb to skin problems.

when it comes to deciding on the type of dog you want and finding out about your prospective pup's background. Buying a puppy is not—or should not be—just another whimsical purchase. This is one instance in which you actually do get to choose your own family! You may be thinking that buying a puppy should be fun—it should not be so serious and so much work. Keep in mind that your puppy is not a cuddly stuffed toy or decorative lawn ornament, but a creature that will become a real member of your family. You will come to realise that, whilst buying a puppy is a pleasurable and exciting endeavour, it is not something to be taken lightly. Relax...the fun will start when the pup comes home!

Always keep in mind that a puppy is nothing more than a baby in a furry disguise...a baby who is virtually helpless in a human world and who trusts his owner for fulfilment of his basic needs for survival. In addition to water and shelter, your pup needs care, protection, guidance and love. If you are not prepared to commit to this, then you are not prepared to own a dog.

Wait a minute, you say. How hard could this be? All of my neighbours own dogs and they seem to be doing just fine. Why should I have to worry about all of this? Well, you should not worry about it; in fact, you will probably find that once your Shih Tzu pup gets used to his new home, he will fall into his place in the family quite naturally. But it never hurts to emphasise the commitment of dog ownership. With some time and patience, it is really not too difficult to raise a curious and exuberant Shih Tzu pup to be a well-adjusted and well-mannered adult dog—a dog that could be your most loyal friend.

PREPARING PUPPY'S PLACE IN YOUR HOME
Researching your breed and finding a breeder are only two aspects of the 'homework' you will have to do before bringing your Shih Tzu puppy home. You will also have to prepare your home and family for the new addition. Much as you would prepare a nursery for a newborn baby, you will need to designate a place in your home that will be the puppy's own. How you prepare your home will depend on how much freedom the dog will be allowed. Whatever you decide, you must ensure that he has a place that he can 'call his own.'

When you bring your new puppy into your home, you are bringing him into what will become his home as well. Obviously, you did not buy a puppy so that he could take over your house, but in order for a puppy to grow into a stable, well-

adjusted dog, he has to feel comfortable in his surroundings. Remember, he is leaving the warmth and security of his mother and littermates, as well as the familiarity of the only place he has ever known, so it is important to

When you bring your new puppy home, your home must be prepared. You'll need a crate, food, toys, collar and lead, food and water bowls, bedding and perhaps other items that your veterinary surgeon might suggest. These things should be purchased prior to the puppy's arrival.

make his transition as easy as possible. By preparing a place in your home for the puppy, you are making him feel as welcome as possible in a strange new place. It should not take him long to get used to it, but the sudden shock of being transplanted is somewhat traumatic for a young pup. Imagine how a small child would feel in the same situation—that is how your puppy must be feeling. It is up to you to reassure him and to let him know, 'Little fellow, you are going to like it here!'

49

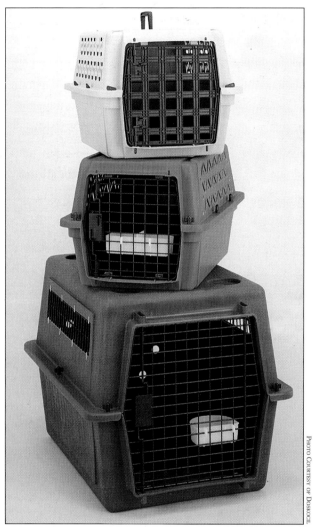

PHOTO COURTESY OF DOSKOCIL.

Your local pet shop should have a wide variety of crates to show you. A medium-size crate is suitable for the puppy and full-grown Shih Tzu.

50

breeders do not advocate crate training, more and more breeders and trainers are recommending crates as a preferred tool for pet puppies as well as show puppies. Crates are not cruel—crates have many humane and highly effective uses in dog care and training. For example, crate training is a very popular and very successful housebreaking method. A crate can keep your dog safe during travel; and, perhaps most importantly, a crate provides your dog with a

WHAT YOU SHOULD BUY
CRATE
To someone unfamiliar with the use of crates in dog training, it may seem like punishment to shut a dog in a crate, but this is not the case at all. Although all

DID YOU KNOW?
During crate training, you should partition off the section of the crate in which the pup stays. If he is given too big an area, this will hinder your training efforts. Crate training is based on the fact that a dog does not like to soil his sleeping quarters, so it is ineffective to keep a pup in a crate that is so big that he can eliminate in one end and get far enough away from it to sleep. Also, you want to make the crate den-like for the pup. Blankets and a favourite toy will make the crate cosy for the small pup; as he grows, you may want to evict some of his 'roommates' to make more room.

It will take some coaxing at first, but be patient. Given some time to get used to it, your pup will adapt to his new home-within-a-home quite nicely.

place of his own in your home. It serves as a 'doggie bedroom' of sorts—your Shih Tzu can curl up in his crate when he wants to sleep or when he just needs a break. Many dogs sleep in their crates overnight. When lined with soft bedding and filled with his favourite toys, a crate becomes a cosy pseudo-den for your dog. Like his ancestors, he too will seek out the comfort and retreat of a den—you just happen to be providing him with something a little more luxurious than his early ancestors enjoyed.

As far as purchasing a crate, the type that you buy is up to you. It will most likely be one of the two most popular types: wire or fibreglass. There are advantages and disadvantages to each type. For example, a wire crate is more open, allowing the air to flow through and affording the dog a view of what is going on around him whilst a fibreglass crate is sturdier. Both can double as travel crates, providing protection for the dog. The size of the crate is another thing to consider. Puppies do not stay puppies forever—in fact, sometimes it seems as if they grow right before your eyes. A Shih Tzu does not grow to be a very large dog, relatively speaking, but he is a substantial dog for his height, which is approximately 10.5 inches. Make sure that the crate you choose

Crates offer many advantages to Shih Tzu owners. Beyond housetraining and travelling, a crate is necessary to keep the dog out of harm's way whenever appropriate.

will accommodate your Shih Tzu both as a pup and as a full-grown dog.

BEDDING
Veterinary bedding in the dog's crate will help the dog feel more at home and you may also like to pop in a small blanket. This will take the place of the leaves,

DID YOU KNOW?
Do not keep an adult dog in a crate for more than ten hours a day. If you keep him crated during the day while you are working, he'll develop into a day-sleeper and a night marauder.

twigs, etc., that the pup would use in the wild to make a den; the pup can make his own 'burrow' in the crate. Although your pup is far removed from his den-making ancestors, the denning instinct is still a part of his genetic makeup. Second, until you bring your pup home, he has been sleeping amidst the warmth of his mother and littermates, and whilst a blanket is not the same as a warm, breathing body, it still provides heat and something with which to snuggle. You will want to wash your pup's bedding frequently in case he has an accident in his crate, and replace or remove any blanket that becomes ragged and starts to fall apart.

Toys

Toys are a must for dogs of all ages, especially for curious playful pups. Puppies are the 'children' of the dog world, and what child does not love toys? Chew toys provide enjoyment to both dog and owner—your dog will enjoy playing with his favourite toys, whilst you will enjoy the fact that they distract him from your expensive shoes and leather sofa. Puppies love to chew; in fact, chewing is a physical need for pups as they are teething, and everything looks appetising! The full range of your possessions—from old dishcloth to Oriental rug—are fair game in the eyes of a

Only offer your puppy toys that have been especially made for dogs. Children's toys are often too soft for the sharp teeth of Shih Tzu puppies. The paint on many of these toys also may be toxic to dogs.

teething pup. Puppies are not all that discerning when it comes to finding something to literally 'sink their teeth into'— everything tastes great!

Shih Tzu puppies are fairly aggressive chewers and only the hardest, strongest toys should be offered to them. Breeders advise owners to resist stuffed toys, because they can become de-stuffed in no time. The overly excited pup may ingest the stuffing, which is neither digestible nor nutritious.

Similarly, squeaky toys are quite popular, but must be avoided for the Shih Tzu. Perhaps a squeaky toy can be used as an aid in training, but not for free play. If a pup 'disembowels' one of these, the small plastic squeaker inside can be dangerous if swallowed. Monitor the condition of all your pup's toys carefully and get rid of any that have been chewed to the point of becoming potentially dangerous.

Be careful of natural bones, which have a tendency to splinter into sharp, dangerous pieces. Also be careful of rawhide, which can turn into pieces that are easy to swallow or into a mushy mess on your carpet.

PHOTO BY MIKKI PET PRODUCTS

TOYS, TOYS, TOYS

With a big variety of dog toys available, and so many that look like they would be a lot of fun for a dog, be careful in your selection. It is amazing what a set of puppy teeth can do to an innocent-looking toy, so, obviously, safety is a major consideration. Be sure to choose the most durable products that you can find. Hard nylon bones and toys are a safe bet, and many of them are offered in different scents and flavours that will be sure to capture your dog's attention. It is always fun to play a game of catch with your dog, and there are balls and flying discs that are specially made to withstand dog teeth.

Your local pet shop usually has a wide variety of dog toys. Try to find toys that are chew resistant since your puppy needs to chew.

53

Pet shops usually stock a wide assortment of leads. Shih Tzu puppies only need light, nylon leads.

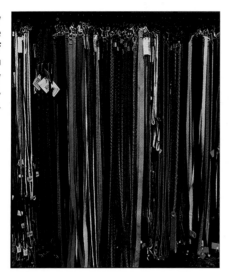

LEAD

A nylon lead is probably the best option as it is the most resistant to puppy teeth should your pup take a liking to chewing on his lead. Of course, this is a habit that should be nipped in the bud, but if your pup likes to chew on his lead he has a very slim chance of being able to chew through the strong nylon. Nylon leads are also lightweight, which is good for a young Shih Tzu who is just getting used to the idea of walking on a lead. For everyday walking and safety purposes, the nylon lead is a good choice. As your pup grows up and gets used to walking on the lead, you may want to purchase a flexible lead. These leads allow you to extend the length to give the dog a broader area to explore or to shorten the length to keep the close to you. Of course there are special thin leads for showing purposes, but these are not sturdy enough for routine walks.

COLLAR

Your pup should get used to wearing a collar all the time since you will want to attach his ID tags to it. You have to attach the lead to something! A lightweight nylon collar is a good choice; make sure that it fits snugly enough so that the pup cannot wriggle out of it, but is loose enough so that it will not be uncomfortably tight around the pup's neck. You should be able to fit a finger between the pup and the collar. It may take some time for your pup to get used to wearing the collar, but soon he will not even notice that it is there.

RESPONSIBILITY...

Grooming tools, collars, leashes, dog beds and, of course, toys will be an expense to you when you first obtain your pup, and the cost will trickle on throughout your dog's lifetime. If your puppy damages or destroys your possessions (as most puppies surely will!) or something belonging to a neighbour, you can calculate additional expense. There is also flea and pest control, which every dog owner faces more than once. You must be able to handle the financial responsibility of owning a dog.

Choose the Appropriate Collar

The BUCKLE COLLAR is the standard collar used for walking your dog. Be sure that you adjust the buckle on growing puppies. Check it every day. It can become too tight overnight! These collars can be made of leather or nylon. Attach your dog's identification tags to this collar.

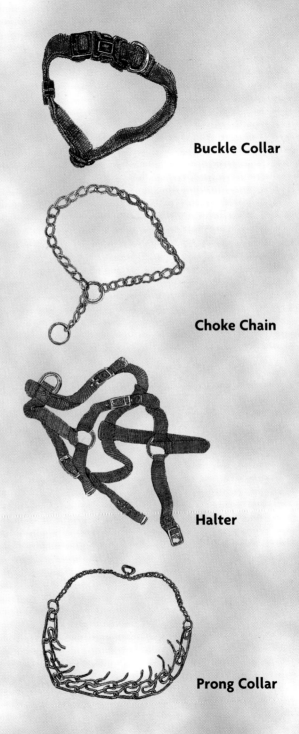

Buckle Collar

The CHOKE CHAIN is the usual collar recommended for training. It is constructed of highly polished steel so that it slides easily through the stainless steel loop. The idea is that the dog controls the pressure around its neck and he will stop pulling if the collar becomes uncomfortable. Never leave a choke collar on your dog when not training.

Choke Chain

The HALTER is for a trained dog that has to be restrained to prevent running away, chasing a cat and the like. Considered the most humane of all collars, it is frequently used on smaller dogs for which collars are not comfortable. The halter is removed when the dog is in the home.

Halter

The PRONG COLLAR certainly appears ominous, like an ancient instrument of torture. Although it is not intended to 'torture' a dog, it is only recommended on the most difficult of dogs, and never on small dogs. It should only be employed by someone who knows how to use it properly.

Prong Collar

Your local pet shop sells an array of dishes and bowls for water and food.

FOOD AND WATER BOWLS

Your pup will need two bowls, one for food and one for water. You may want two sets of bowls, one for inside and one for outside, depending on where the dog will be fed and where he will be spending most of his time. Stainless steel or sturdy plastic bowls are popular choices. Plastic bowls are more chewable. Dogs tend not to chew on the steel variety, which can be sterilised. It is important to buy sturdy bowls since anything is in danger of being chewed by puppy teeth and you do not want your dog to be constantly chewing apart his bowl (for his safety and for your purse!).

CLEANING SUPPLIES

Until a pup is housetrained you will be doing a lot of cleaning. Accidents will occur, which

PUPPY PROOFING

Thoroughly puppy-proof your house before bringing your puppy home. Never use roach or rodent poisons in any area accessible to the puppy. Avoid the use of toilet bowl cleaners. Most dogs are born with toilet bowl sonar and will take a drink if the lid is left open. Also keep the trash secured and out of reach.

CHEMICAL TOXINS

Scour your carport for potential puppy dangers. Remove weed killers, pesticides and antifreeze materials. Antifreeze is highly toxic and even a few drops can kill an adult dog. The sweet taste attracts the animal, who will quickly consume it from the floor or curbside.

It is your responsibility to clean up after your dog has relieved himself. Pet shops have various aids to assist in the cleanup job.

is okay in the beginning because the puppy does not know any better. All you can do is be prepared to clean up any 'accidents.' Old rags, towels, newspapers and a safe disinfectant are good to have on hand.

BEYOND THE BASICS

The items previously discussed are the bare necessities. You will find out what else you need as you go along—grooming supplies, flea/tick protection, baby gates to partition a room, etc. These things will vary depending on your situation but it is important that you have everything you need to feed and make your Shih Tzu comfortable in his first few days at home.

PUPPY-PROOFING YOUR HOME

Aside from making sure that your Shih Tzu will be comfortable in your home, you also have to make sure that your home is safe for

your Shih Tzu. This means taking precautions that your pup will not get into anything he should not get into and that there is nothing within his reach that may harm him should he sniff it, chew it, inspect it, etc. This probably seems obvious since, whilst you are primarily concerned with your

NATURAL TOXINS

Examine your lawn and garden landscaping before bringing your puppy home. Many varieties of plants have leaves, stems or flowers that are toxic if ingested, and you can depend on a curious puppy to investigate them. Ask your veterinarian for information on poisonous plants or research them at your library.

pup's safety, at the same time you do not want your belongings to be ruined. Breakables should be placed out of reach if your dog is to have full run of the house. If he is to be limited to certain places within the house, keep any potentially dangerous items in the 'off-limits' areas. An electrical cord can pose a danger should the puppy decide to taste it—and who is going to convince a pup that it would not make a great chew toy? Cords should be fastened tightly against the wall. If your dog is going to spend time in a crate, make sure that there is nothing near his crate that he can reach if he sticks his curious little nose or paws through the openings. Just as you would with a child, keep all household cleaners and

DID YOU KNOW?

Taking your dog from the breeder to your home in a car can be a very uncomfortable experience for both of you. The puppy will have been taken from his warm, friendly, safe environment and brought into a strange new environment. An environment that moves! Be prepared for loose bowels, urination, crying, whining and even fear biting. With proper love and encouragement when you arrive home, the stress of the trip should quickly disappear.

DID YOU KNOW?

It will take at least two weeks for your puppy to become accustomed to his new surroundings. Give him lots of love, attention, handling, frequent opportunities to relieve himself, a diet he likes to eat and a place he can call his own.

chemicals where the pup cannot get to them.

It is also important to make sure that the outside of your home is safe. Of course your puppy should never be unsupervised, but a pup let loose in the garden will want to run and explore, and he should be granted that freedom. Do not let a fence give you a false sense of security; you would be surprised how crafty (and persistent) a dog can be in figuring out how to dig under and squeeze his way through small holes, or to jump or climb over a fence. The remedy is to make the fence high enough so that it really is impossible for your dog to get over it (about 3 metres should suffice), and well embedded into the ground. Be sure to repair or secure any gaps in the fence. Check the fence periodically to ensure that it is in good shape and make repairs as needed; a very determined pup may return to the same spot to 'work on it' until he is able to get through.

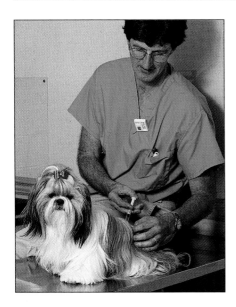

FIRST TRIP TO THE VET

You have picked out your puppy, and your home and family are ready. Now all you have to do is collect your Shih Tzu from the breeder and the fun begins, right? Well...not so fast. Something else you need to prepare is your pup's first trip to the veterinary surgeon. Perhaps the breeder can recommend someone in the area that specialises in Shih Tzu, or maybe you know some other Shih Tzu owners who can suggest a good vet. Either way, you should have an appointment arranged for your pup before you pick him up and plan on taking him for an examination before bringing him home.

The pup's first visit will consist of an overall examination to make sure that the pup does not have any problems that are not apparent to the eye. The veterinary surgeon will also set up a schedule for the pup's vaccinations; the breeder will inform you of which ones the pup has already received and the vet can continue from there.

INTRODUCTION TO THE FAMILY

Everyone in the house will be excited about the puppy coming home and will want to pet him and play with him, but it is best to make the introduction low-key so as not to overwhelm the puppy. He is apprehensive already. It is the first time he has been separated from his mother and the breeder, and the ride to your home is likely the first time he has been in an auto. The last thing you want to do is smother him, as this will only frighten him further. This is not to say that human contact is not extremely necessary at this stage, because this is the time when

You should have your dog examined regularly by your local veterinary surgeon. Your adult Shih Tzu's booster vaccinations should coincide with his physical examination.

> **DID YOU KNOW?**
>
> You will probably start feeding your pup the same food that he has been getting from the breeder; the breeder should give you a few days' supply to start you off. Although you should not give your pup too many treats, you will want to have puppy treats on hand for coaxing, training, rewards, etc. Be careful, though, as a small pup's calorie requirements are relatively low and a few treats can add up to almost a full day's worth of calories without the required nutrition.

a connection between the pup and his human family is formed. Gentle petting and soothing words should help console him, as well as just putting him down and letting him explore on his own (under your watchful eye, of course).

The pup may approach the family members or may busy himself with exploring for a while. Gradually, each person should spend some time with the pup, one at a time, crouching down to get as close to the pup's level as possible and letting him sniff their hands and petting him gently. He definitely needs human attention and he needs to be touched—this is how to form an immediate bond. Just remember that the pup is experiencing a lot of things for the first time, at the same time. There are new people, new noises, new smells, and new things

to investigate: so be gentle, be affectionate, and be as comforting as you can be.

YOUR PUP'S FIRST NIGHT HOME
You have travelled home with your new charge safely in his basket or crate. He's been to the vet for a thorough check-over; he's been weighed, his papers examined; perhaps he's even been vaccinated and wormed as well. He's met the family, licked the whole family, including the excited children and the less-than-happy cat. He's explored his area, his new bed, the garden and anywhere else he's been permitted. He's eaten his first meal at home and relieved himself in the proper place. He's heard lots of new sounds, smelled new friends and seen more of the outside world than ever before.

The puppies have been socialised to their own brothers and sisters. The socialisation process with people must continue as the puppy grows up.

That was just the first day! He's worn out and is ready for bed…or so you think!

It's puppy's first night and you are ready to say 'Good night'—keep in mind that this is puppy's first night ever to be sleeping alone. His dam and littermates are no longer at paw's length and he's a bit scared, cold and lonely. Be reassuring to your new family member. This is not the time to spoil him and give in to his inevitable whining.

Puppies whine. They whine to let the others know where they are and hopefully to get company out of it. Place your pup in his new bed or crate in his room and close the door. Mercifully, he may fall asleep without a peep. If the inevitable occurs, ignore the whining: he is fine. Be strong and keep his interest in mind. Do not allow your heart to become guilty and visit the pup. He will fall asleep.

Many breeders recommend placing a piece of bedding from his former homestead in his new bed so that he recognises the scent of his littermates. Others still advise placing a hot water bottle in his bed for warmth. This latter may be a good idea provided the pup doesn't attempt to suckle—he'll get good and wet and may not fall asleep so fast.

Puppy's first night can be somewhat stressful for the pup and his new family. Remember that you are setting the tone of nighttime at your house. Unless you want to play with your pup every evening at 10

Don't overwhelm the puppy. Give your new Shih Tzu baby time to adjust to the family and activity of the household. Provide a cosy bed in which he can sleep or just take a break.

p.m., midnight and 2 a.m., don't initiate the habit. Your family will thank you, and so will your pup!

PREVENTING PUPPY PROBLEMS
SOCIALISATION
Now that you have done all of the preparatory work and have helped your pup get accustomed to his new home and family, it is about time for you to have some fun! Socialising your Shih Tzu pup gives you the opportunity to show off your new friend, and your pup gets to reap the benefits of being an adorable furry creature that people will want to pet and, in general, think is absolutely precious!

Besides getting to know his new family, your puppy should be exposed to other people, animals and situations, but of course he must not come into close contact with dogs you don't know well until his course of injections is fully complete. This will help him become well adjusted as he grows manifest itself in fear and aggression as the dog grows up. He needs lots of human contact, affection, handling and exposure to other animals.

Once your pup has received his necessary vaccinations, feel free to take him out and about (on his lead, of course). Walk him around the neighbourhood, take him on your daily errands, let people pet him, let him meet other dogs and pets, etc. Puppies do not have to try to make friends; there will be no shortage of people who will want to introduce themselves. Just make sure that you carefully supervise each meeting. If the neighbourhood children want to say hello, for example, that is great—children and pups most often make great companions. Sometimes an excited child can unintentionally handle a pup too roughly, or an overzealous pup can playfully nip a little too hard. You want to make socialisation experiences positive ones. What a pup learns during this very formative stage will impact his attitude toward future encounters. You want your dog to be comfortable around everyone. A pup that has a bad experience with a child may grow up to be a dog that is shy around or aggressive toward children.

up and less prone to being timid or fearful of the new things he will encounter. Your pup's socialisation began at the breeder's but now it is your responsibility to continue it. The socialisation he receives up until the age of 12 weeks is the most critical, as this is the time when he forms his impressions of the outside world. Be especially careful during the eight-to-ten-week period, also known as the fear period. The interaction he receives during this time should be gentle and reassuring. Lack of socialisation can

Dog beds come in all sizes and shapes. This is a dog castle where the puppies have a cave-like place in which to sleep. It is important that the covering of the bed can easily be washed.

DID YOU KNOW?

An important consideration to be discussed is the sex of your puppy. For a family companion, a bitch may be the better choice, considering the female's inbred concern for all young creatures and her accompanying tolerance and patience. It is always advised to spay a pet bitch, which may guarantee her a longer life.

CONSISTENCY IN TRAINING

Dogs, being pack animals, naturally need a leader, or else they try to establish dominance in their packs. When you bring a dog into your family, the choice of who becomes the leader and who becomes the 'pack' is entirely up to you! Your pup's intuitive quest for dominance, coupled with the fact that it is nearly impossible to look at an adorable Shih Tzu pup, with his 'puppy-dog' eyes, and not cave in, give the pup almost an unfair advantage in getting the upper hand! A pup will definitely test the waters to see what he can and cannot do. Do not give in to those pleading eyes—stand your ground when it comes to disciplining the pup and make sure that all family members do the same. It will only confuse the pup when Mother tells him to get off the couch when he is used to sitting up there with Father to watch the

nightly news. Avoid discrepancies by having all members of the household decide on the rules before the pup even comes home...and be consistent in enforcing them! Early training shapes the dog's personality, so you cannot be unclear in what you expect.

COMMON PUPPY PROBLEMS

The best way to prevent puppy problems is to be proactive in stopping an undesirable behaviour as soon as it starts. The old saying 'You can't teach an old dog new tricks' does not necessarily hold true, but it is true that it is much easier to discourage bad behaviour in a young developing pup than to wait until the pup's

DID YOU KNOW?

Training your puppy takes much patience and can be frustrating at times, but you should see results from your efforts. If you have a puppy that seems untrainable, take him to a trainer or behaviourist. The dog may have a personality problem that requires the help of a professional, or perhaps you need help in learning how to train your dog.

bad behaviour becomes the adult dog's bad habit. There are some problems that are especially prevalent in puppies as they develop.

Young puppies, just a few days old, know how to whine and cry when they are hungry or uncomfortable. Puppies will try hard to tell you how they feel.

NIPPING

As puppies start to teethe, they feel the need to sink their teeth into anything available…unfortunately that includes your fingers, arms, hair, and toes. You may find this behaviour cute for the first five seconds…until you feel just how sharp those puppy teeth are. This is something you want to discourage immediately and consistently with a firm 'No!' (or whatever number of firm 'No's it takes for him to understand that you mean business). Then replace your finger with an appropriate chew toy. Whilst this behaviour is merely annoying when the dog is young, it can become dangerous as your Shih Tzu's adult teeth grow in and his jaws develop, and he continues to think it is okay

to gnaw on human appendages. Your Shih Tzu does not mean any harm with a friendly nip, but he also does not know his own strength.

DID YOU KNOW?

Chewing goes hand in hand with nipping in the sense that a teething puppy is always looking for a way to soothe his aching gums. In this case, instead of chewing on you, he may have taken a liking to your favourite shoe or something else which he should not be chewing. Again, realise that this is a normal canine behaviour that does not need to be discouraged, only redirected. Your pup just needs to be taught what is acceptable to chew on and what is off limits. Consistently tell him NO when you catch him chewing on something forbidden and give him a chew toy. Conversely, praise him when you catch him chewing on something appropriate. In this way you are discouraging the inappropriate behaviour and reinforcing the desired behaviour. The puppy chewing should stop after his adult teeth have come in, but an adult dog continues to chew for various reasons—perhaps because he is bored, perhaps to relieve tension or perhaps he just likes to chew. That is why it is important to redirect his chewing when he is still young.

CRYING/WHINING

Your pup will often cry, whine, whimper, howl or make some type of commotion when he is left alone. This is basically his way of calling out for attention to make sure that you know he is there and that you have not forgotten about him. He feels insecure when he is left alone, when you are out of the house and he is in his crate or when you are in another part of the house and he cannot see you. The noise he is making is an expression of the anxiety he feels at being alone, so he needs to be taught that being alone is okay. You are not actually training the dog to stop making noise, you are training him to feel comfortable when he is alone and thus removing the need for him to make the noise. This is where the crate filled with cosy bedding and a favourite toy comes in handy. You want to know that he is safe when you are not there to supervise, and you know that he will be safe in his crate rather than roaming freely about the house. In order for the pup to stay in his crate without making a fuss, he needs to be comfortable in his crate. On that note, it is extremely important that the crate is never used as a form of punishment, or the pup will have a negative association with the crate.

Accustom the pup to the crate in short, gradually increasing time intervals in which you put him in the crate, maybe with a treat, and stay in the room with him. If he cries or

makes a fuss, do not go to him, but stay in his sight. Gradually he will realise that staying in his crate is all right without your help, and it will not be so traumatic for him when you are not around. You may want to leave the radio on softly when you leave the house; the sound of human voices may be comforting to him.

Your wisest investment will be your Shih Tzu's crate. Introduce the puppy to the crate in small intervals, gradually increasing the amount of time he's expected to stay.

DID YOU KNOW?

The majority of problems that are commonly seen in young pups will disappear as your dog gets older. However, how you deal with problems when he is young will determine how he reacts to discipline as an adult dog. It is important to establish who is boss (hopefully it will be you!) right away when you are first bonding wiith your dog. This bond will set the tone for the rest of your life together.

DIETARY AND FEEDING CONSIDERATIONS

Today the choices of food for your Shih Tzu are many and varied. There are simply dozens of brands of food in all sorts of flavours and textures, ranging from puppy diets to those for seniors. There are even hypoallergenic and low-calorie diets available. Because your Shih Tzu's food has a bearing on coat, health and temperament, it is essential that the most suitable diet is selected for a Shih Tzu of his age. It is fair to say, however, that even dedicated owners can be somewhat perplexed by the enormous range of foods available. Only understanding what is best for your dog will help you reach a valued decision.

Dog foods are produced in three basic types: dried, semi-moist and tinned. Dried foods are useful for the cost-conscious for overall they tend to be less expensive than semi-moist or tinned. These contain the least fat and the most preservatives.

DID YOU KNOW?

A good test for proper diet is the colour, odour, and firmness of your dog's stool. A healthy dog usually produces three semi-hard stools per day. The stools should have no unpleasant odour. They should be the same colour from excretion to excretion.

In general tinned foods are made up of 60–70 percent water, whilst semi-moist ones often contain so much sugar that they are perhaps the least preferred by owners, even though their dogs seem to like them.

When selecting your dog's diet, three stages of development must be considered: the puppy stage, adult stage and the senior or veteran stage.

DID YOU KNOW?

You must store your dry dog food carefully. Open packages of dog food quickly lose their vitamin value, usually within 90 days of being opened. Mould spores and vermin could also contaminate the food.

PUPPY STAGE

Puppies instinctively want to suck milk from their mother's teats and a normal puppy will exhibit this behaviour from just a few moments following birth. If puppies do not attempt to suckle within the first half-hour or so, they should be encouraged to do so by placing them on a nipple,

FOOD PREFERENCE

Selecting the best dry dog food is difficult. There is no majority consensus among veterinary scientists as to the value of nutrient analyses (protein, fat, fibre, moisture, ash, cholesterol, minerals, etc.). All agree that feeding trials are what matters, but you also have to consider the individual dog. Its weight, age, activity and what pleases its taste, all must be considered. It is probably best to take the advice of your veterinary surgeon. Every dog's dietary requirements vary, even during the lifetime of a particular dog.

It your dog is fed a good dry food, it does not require supplements of meat or vegetables. Dogs do appreciate a little variety in their diets so you may choose to stay with the same brand, but vary the flavour. Alternatively you may wish to add a little flavoured stock to give a difference to the taste.

---

having selected ones with plenty of milk. This early milk supply is important in providing colostrum to protect the puppies during the first eight to ten weeks of their lives. Although a mother's milk is much better than any milk formula, despite there being some excellent ones available, if the puppies do not feed you will have to feed them yourself. For those with less experience, advice from a veterinary surgeon is important so that you feed not only the right quantity of milk but that of correct quality, fed at suitably frequent intervals, usually every two hours during the first few days of life.

Puppies should be allowed to nurse from their mothers for about the first six weeks, although from the third or fourth week you will have begun to introduce small portions of suitable solid food. Most breeders like to introduce alternate

Puppy diets should be well balanced so that additional vitamins, minerals and supplements are not necessary.

Not all puppies can tolerate cow's or goat's milk. Never substitute milk for water, which your puppy will need during the day.

milk and meat meals initially, building up to weaning time.

By the time the puppies are seven or a maximum of eight weeks old, they should be fully weaned and fed solely on a proprietary puppy food. Selection of the most suitable, good-quality diet at this time is essential for a puppy's fastest growth rate is during the first year of life. Veterinary surgeons are usually able to offer advice in this regard and, although the frequency of meals will have been reduced over time, only when a young dog has reached the age of about 18 months should an adult diet be fed.

Puppy and junior diets should be well balanced for the needs of your dog, so that except in certain

circumstances additional vitamins, minerals and proteins will not be required.

ADULT DIETS
A dog is considered an adult when it has stopped growing, so in general the diet of a Shih Tzu can be changed to an adult one at about 18 months of age. Again you should rely upon your veterinary surgeon or dietary specialist to recommend an acceptable maintenance diet. Major dog food manufacturers specialise in this type of food, and it is just necessary for you to select the one best suited to your dog's needs. Active dogs may have different requirements than sedate dogs.

SENIOR DIETS
As dogs get older, their metabolism changes. The older dog usually exercises less, moves more slowly and sleeps more. This change in lifestyle and physiological performance requires a change in diet. Since these changes take place slowly, they might not be recognisable. What is easily recognisable is weight gain. By continuing to feed your dog an adult-maintenance diet when it is slowing down metabolically, your dog will gain weight. Obesity in an older dog compounds the health problems that already accompany old age.

As your dog gets older, few of his organs function up to par. The

Once your Shih Tzu is completely housetrained, water should be available to him at all times.

kidneys slow down and the intestines become less efficient. These age-related factors are best handled with a change in diet and a change in feeding schedule to give smaller portions that are more easily digested.

There is no single best diet for every older dog. Whilst many dogs do well on light or senior diets, other dogs do better on puppy diets or other special premium diets such as lamb and rice. Be sensitive to your senior Shih Tzu's diet and this will help control other problems that may arise with your old friend.

WATER

Just as your dog needs proper nutrition from his food, water is an essential 'nutrient' as well. Water keeps the dog's body properly hydrated and promotes

GRAIN-BASED DIETS

Many adult diets are based on grain. There is nothing wrong with this as long as it does not contain soy meal. Diets based on soy often cause flatulence (passing gas).

Grain-based diets are almost always the least expensive and a good grain diet is just as good as the most expensive diet containing animal protein.

There are many cases, however, when your dog might require a special diet. These special requirements should only be recommended by your veterinary surgeon.

69

normal function of the body's systems. During housebreaking it is necessary to keep an eye on how much water your Shih Tzu is drinking, but once he is reliably trained he should have access to clean fresh water at all times. Make sure that the dog's water bowl is clean, and change the water often, making sure that water is always available for your dog, especially if you feed dried food.

EXERCISE

Although a Shih Tzu is small, all dogs require some form of exercise, regardless of breed. A sedentary lifestyle is as harmful to a dog as it is to a person. The Shih Tzu is a fairly active breed that enjoys exercise, but you don't have to be an Olympic athlete! Regular walks, play sessions in the garden, or letting the dog run free in the garden under your supervision are sufficient forms of exercise for the Shih Tzu. For those who are more ambitious, you will find that your Shih Tzu also enjoys long walks or perhaps an occasional hike. Bear in mind that an overweight dog should never be suddenly over-exercised;

Read the label on your dog food. Most Manufacturers merely advise you of 50-55% of the contents, leaving the other 45% in doubt.

instead he should be allowed to increase exercise slowly. Not only is exercise essential to keep the dog's body fit, it is essential to his mental well being. A bored dog will find something to do, which often manifests itself in some type of destructive behaviour. In this sense, it is essential for the owner's mental well being as well!

GROOMING

Your Shih Tzu will need to be groomed regularly, so it is essential that short grooming sessions are introduced from a

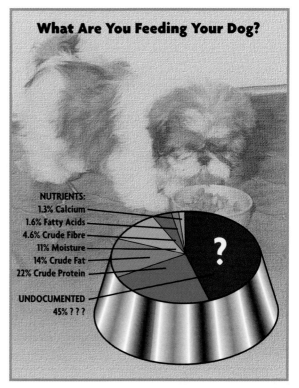

What Are You Feeding Your Dog?

NUTRIENTS:
1.3% Calcium
1.6% Fatty Acids
4.6% Crude Fibre
11% Moisture
14% Crude Fat
22% Crude Protein

UNDOCUMENTED
45% ? ? ?

?

very early age. From the very beginning, a few minutes each day should be set aside for grooming. Increase the duration of the sessions, building up slowly as the puppy matures and the coat grows in length. Your puppy should be taught to stand on a solid surface for grooming; a suitable table is one on which the dog will not slip. Under no circumstances should you leave your Shih Tzu alone on a table, for he may all too easily jump off and injure himself.

When the puppy is used to standing on the table, you will need to teach him to be rolled over onto his side. Do this by grasping his front and back legs on the opposite side of your own body, then gently placing him down by leaning over him for reassurance. To begin, just stroke his tummy so that he looks upon this new routine as something highly pleasurable. Then, when you know he is comfortable with this, introduce a few gentle brush strokes. Be sure you don't tug at any knots at this stage, for this would cause

him to associate this routine with pain. This may take a little getting used to both for you and your puppy, but only if your Shih Tzu learns to lie down on his side will you easily be able to groom in all the awkward places. You will both be glad you had a little patience to learn this trick from the very start!

You will notice that not only does your Shih Tzu's coat grow longer with age but also, usually between 10 and 12 months of age, the coat changes from a puppy coat to an adult one. This will be a

As your Shih Tzu puppy is growing into his coat, you will have to decide whether to trim him in a 'pet clip' or to maintain the full-length coat that gives the breed its fame! Keep the dog's comfort and your time commitment in mind.

71

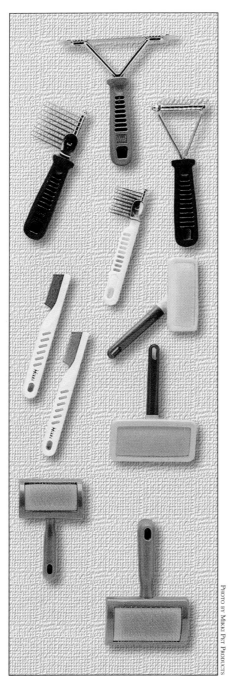

Your local pet shop will have a variety of grooming tools, brushes and combs which will assist you in keeping your Shih Tzu's coat in peak condition.

difficult time, for knots will form very easily and you will realise how comparatively easy grooming your youngster was!

You will certainly need to groom the coat between bath times, but never groom the coat when completely dry. To avoid breaking the ends, use a light conditioning spray. Even water dispensed from a fine-spray bottle is better than no moisture at all.

ROUTINE GROOMING

With your Shih Tzu lying on his side, the coat should be parted, layered and brushed section by section, always in the direction of the coat growth. It is imperative to groom right down to the skin so

GROOMING SUPPLIES

How much grooming equipment you purchase will depend on how much grooming you are going to do. Here are some basics:

- Natural bristle brush
- Slicker brush
- Metal comb
- Scissors
- Blaster
- Rubber mat
- Dog shampoo
- Spray hose attachment
- Ear cleaner
- Cotton wipes
- Towels
- Nail clippers

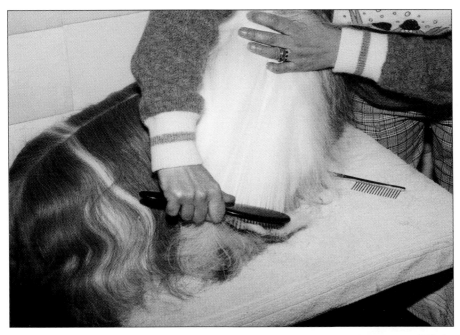

The Shih Tzu should be brushed, section by section, in the direction of the hair growth.

that the undercoat is not left matted. After using a good-quality bristle brush, a wide-toothed comb can be used to finish each section.

If you do find matts in your Shih Tzu's coat, spray the matt with a generous amount of conditioning or anti-tangle spray. Leave this to soak in for a few moments, then gently tease out the matt with your fingers. Always work from the inside out, or the knot will just get tighter! Tight knots will probably need to be teased out using a wide-toothed comb, but be careful not to tug at the knot. It will be painful for the pup, and will also pull out too much coat.

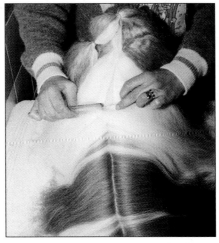

A wide-toothed comb can be used after the coat has been brushed.

Take care in grooming the tummy and under the 'arm-pits,' for these areas are especially sensitive. There is really no harm in cutting away small tight knots

73

from under the armpits, as these will not show and the dog will feel more comfortable. However, a Shih Tzu in show coat should not be trimmed, so scissors should only be used when absolutely necessary. Trimming below the pads of the feet prevents uncomfortable hairballs forming between the pads. On males, most owners also trim off a little hair from the end of the penis, but a good half inch or a few centimetres must be left so that tiny hairs to not aggravate the penis and set up infection. Whatever you do, take care not to cut through a nipple—-and remember that males have little nipples too!

Legs and trousers of a Shih Tzu are very heavily coated and will also need regular grooming. To prevent knots and tangles, be sure to immediately remove any debris that may have accumulated following a visit outdoors. Also always check your dog's back end to see that nothing remains attached to the coat from his toilet. Between baths you may like to use a damp sponge, but always be sure to dry the coat thoroughly. Drying will keep your Shih Tzu comfortable and will prevent the coat from curling too much.

Some Shih Tzu don't seem to mind having their feet groomed, while others hate it. Nonetheless, you will have to check the feet thoroughly on a regular basis. Be sure you don't allow knots to build up between the toes, and always keep an eye on the length of the toenails.

HEAD, TOP-KNOT AND THE FINISHING TOUCHES

It is essential to keep the whiskers, beard and eyes of a Shih Tzu clean, so these must be checked every day. Eyes can be cleaned with a canine liquid eye cleaner. The beard and whiskers can be washed and combed through, and some owners find it useful to attach elastic on each side of the beard to prevent soiling, especially when the dog is eating.

When grooming, pay special attention to the hair behind the ear. This hair is often of a finer texture and knots easily. From about five months of age, your Shih Tzu will have enough head hair to tie into a top-knot. Comb up the hair from the stop, and fix it into a tiny elastic band. Most owners use dental elastics, but take care not to pull up the hair too tightly so that it pulls on the eyes. Elastics will generally need to be changed at least once a day. Never pull them out; instead, always cut them carefully with scissors so as not to damage any hair. Under no circumstances should the head hair of a Shih Tzu be trimmed for the show ring, although if a Shih Tzu is maintained in a pet trim the head hair can be cut short to match the rest of the coat. Some pet owners, though, like to keep long fringing on the ears.

When grooming is complete, use a wide-toothed comb to create a straight parting down the length of the back, so that the coat falls evenly on either side.

BATHING AND DRYING

How frequently you decide to bathe your Shih Tzu will depend very much on whether your dog is a show dog or a pet. Show dogs are usually bathed before every show, which may be as frequent as once a week. Pet dogs are usually bathed less frequently, especially if they are kept in puppy trim because the coat does not drag on the ground to pick up dirt and debris.

Every owner has his or her own preference as to how best to bathe, but ideally the coat should be groomed through before bathing. I like to stand my own dogs on a non-slip mat in the bath, then wet the coat thoroughly using a shower. It is imperative that the water temperature is tested on your own hand before spraying the dog. Use a good quality shampoo designed especially for dogs, always stroking it into the coat rather than rubbing, so as not to create knots. When the shampoo has been thoroughly rinsed out, apply a canine conditioner in the same

The dog should be soaked thoroughly before the shampoo is applied. Only use shampoo made especially for dogs. Human shampoo is too strong and removes protective oils from the dog's skin.

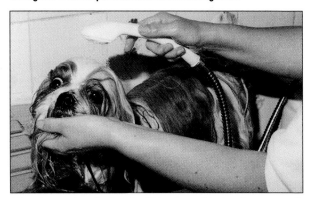

After shampooing, the dog should be thoroughly rinsed to remove all of the soap and dirt from the dog's coat.

After the dog has been thoroughly rinsed, wrap him in an absorbent bath towel and help him out of the tub. Once you release him he'll shake the water from his coat.

Use a blaster to dry his coat as thoroughly as possible. Never let your Shih Tzu dry naturally!

Don't forget to do the belly region. Lay the dog on his back in your lap and use a blaster at very low speed.

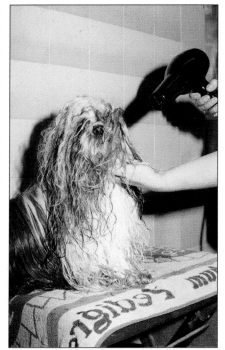

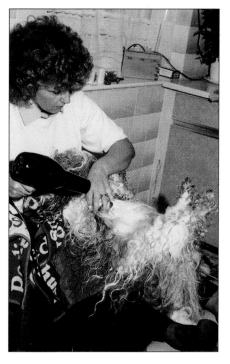

DID YOU KNOW?

Once you are sure that the dog is thoroughly rinsed, squeeze the excess water out of the coat with your hand and dry him with a heavy towel. You should use a blaster on his coat, not just let it dry naturally. In cold weather, never allow your dog outside with a wet coat.

There are 'dry bath' products on the market, which are sprays and powders intended for spot cleaning, that can be used between regular baths, if necessary. They are not substitutes for regular baths, but they are easy to use for touch-ups as they do not require rinsing.

manner, then rinse again until the water runs clear. Many people like to use a baby shampoo on the head to avoid irritation to the eyes, and some like to plug the ears with cotton wool to avoid water getting inside them. Personally, I use neither of these. By just taking special care in those areas, I have never encountered problems.

Before taking your dog out of the bath, it is a good idea to use a highly absorbent cloth to soak up excess moisture. You can then lift your Shih Tzu out of the bath, wrapped in a clean towel. Undoubtedly your dog

Once the dog's coat is reasonably dry, start brushing it out.

will want to shake—so be prepared!

Drying can be done on the same table you use for the grooming process. Work systematically, all the while brushing as well as applying warm air from the hair-dryer. Never just blow-dry the dog with the intention of grooming later, or your Shih Tzu's coat will not end up in good condition. Certainly you should never allow a Shih Tzu to dry naturally.

Put the finishing touches to your dog's coat, just as you would have done if grooming without a bath. Bathing and grooming a long-coated breed is always a lengthy task, but I assure you the end result will have made it all worthwhile.

DID YOU KNOW?

The use of human soap products like shampoo, bubble bath and hand soap can be damaging to a dog's coat and skin. Human products are too strong and remove the protective oils coating the dog's hair and skin (making him water-resistant). Use only shampoo made especially for dogs and you may like to use a medicated shampoo which will always help to keep external parasites at bay.

This Shih Tzu has been put down in oil. After the bath, some groomers apply a mineral, vegetable or baby oil to the coat, working it from the roots to the ends of the hairs. This treatment to improve the coat is followed by hot towels or the blaster. Of course, the oil must be bathed out after several minutes.

EAR CLEANING

Because the Shih Tzu has such a long coat, long hair will also grow inside the ears. This should be carefully plucked out either with special blunt-ended tweezers or, if you prefer, with your fingertips. If you always remove only a few hairs at a time, this should be entirely painless.

Ears should be kept clean. Ears can be cleaned with a cotton wool bud and special cleaner or ear powder made especially for dogs. Be on the lookout for any signs of infection or ear mite infestation. If your Shih Tzu has been shaking his head or scratching at his ears frequently, this usually indicates a problem. If his ears have an unusual odour, this is a sure sign of mite infestation or infection, and a signal to have his ears checked by the veterinary surgeon.

NAIL CLIPPING

Your Shih Tzu should be accustomed to having his nails trimmed at an early age, since it will be part of your maintenance routine throughout his life. Long nails can all too easily get caught in the Shih Tzu's long coat, and can be sharp if they scratch someone unintentionally. Also, a long nail has a better chance of ripping and bleeding, or causing the feet to spread. A good rule of thumb is that if you can hear your dog's nails clicking on the floor when he walks, his nails are too long.

Before you start cutting, make sure you can identify the 'quick' in each nail. The quick is a blood vessel that runs through

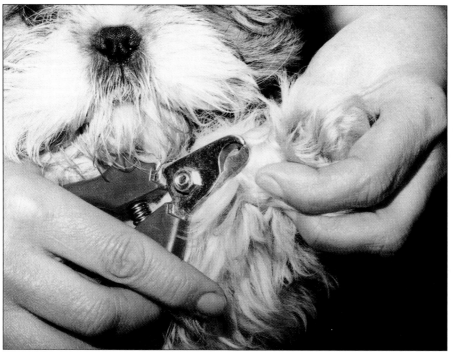

The nails should be carefully clipped with special dog nail clippers. Accustom your Shih Tzu to this from puppyhood and you will have a more cooperative adult.

the centre of each nail and grows rather close to the end. It will bleed if accidentally cut, which will be quite painful for the dog as it contains nerve endings. Keep some type of clotting agent on hand, such as a styptic pencil or styptic powder (the type used for shaving). This will stop the bleeding quickly when applied to the end of the cut nail. Do not panic if this happens, just stop the bleeding and talk soothingly to your dog. Once he has calmed down, move on to the next nail. It is better to clip a little at a time, particularly with black-nailed dogs.

The excess hair in the ears should be carefully plucked with a blunt-ended tweezers (or your fingertips).

79

The hair growing on the bottom of the Shih Tzu's foot, around the pad, should be trimmed short.

Canine Pedicure

Nail Casing

Quick

Cut Line

Dark-Coloured Nail

Light-Coloured Nail

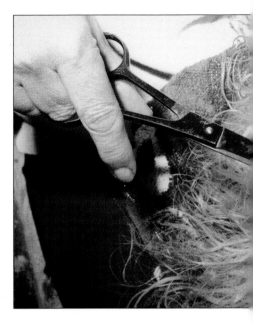

Hold your pup steady as you begin trimming his nails; you do not want him to make any sudden movements or run away. Talk to him soothingly and stroke him as you clip. Holding his foot in your hand, simply take off the end of each nail in one quick clip. You can purchase nail clippers that are specially made for dogs; you can probably find them wherever you buy pet or grooming supplies.

TRAVELLING WITH YOUR DOG
CAR TRAVEL
You should accustom your Shih Tzu to riding in a car at an early age. You may or may not take him in the car often, but at the very least he will need to go to the vet and you do not want these trips to be traumatic for the dog or a big

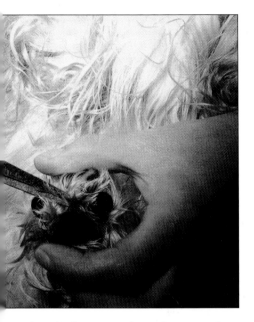

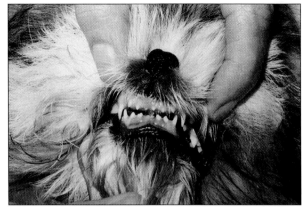

The teeth of a puppy Shih Tzu.

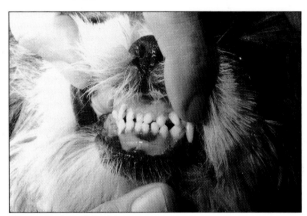

The teeth of an adult Shih Tzu.

hassle for you. The safest way for a dog to ride in the car is in his crate. If he uses a crate in the house, you can use the same crate for travel.

Put the pup in the crate and see how he reacts. If he seems uneasy, you can have a passenger hold him on his lap whilst you drive. Another option is a specially made safety harness for dogs, which straps the dog in much like a seat belt. Do not let the dog roam loose in the vehicle—this is very dangerous! If you should stop short, your dog can be thrown and injured. If the dog starts climbing on you and pestering you whilst you are driving, you will not be able to concentrate on the road. It is an unsafe situation for everyone—human and canine.

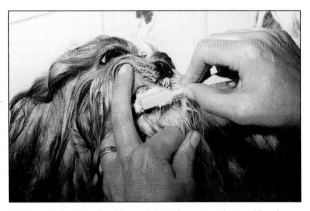

Brush your dog's teeth with special tooth paste and a toothbrush that is made for dogs.

For long trips, be prepared to stop to let the dog relieve himself. Bring along whatever you need to clean up after him. You should take along some paper kitchen towels and perhaps some old towelling for use should he have an accident in the car or suffer from travel sickness.

AIR TRAVEL

Whilst it is possible to take a dog on a flight within Britain, this is fairly unusual and advance permission is always required. The dog will be required to travel in a fibreglass crate and you should always check in advance with the airline regarding specific requirements. To help the dog be at ease, put one of his favourite toys in the crate with him. Do not feed the dog for at least six hours before the trip to minimise his need to relieve himself. However, certain regulations specify that water must always be made available to the dog in the crate.

When travelling with your Shih Tzu in a car, keep him in his crate. This is the safest, most acceptable way of travelling with a dog.

> **TRAVEL TIP**
> When travelling, never let your dog off-lead in a strange area. Your dog could run away out of fear or decide to chase a passing chipmunk or cat or simply want to stretch his legs without restriction—you might never see your canine friend again.

> **TRAVEL TIP**
> If you are going on a long motor trip with your dog, be sure the hotels are dog friendly. Many hotels do not accept dogs. Also take along some ice that can be thawed and offered to your dog if he becomes overheated. Most dogs like to lick ice.

TRAVEL TIP

Never leave your dog alone in the car. In hot weather your dog can die from the high temperature inside a closed vehicle; even a car parked in the shade can heat up very quickly. Leaving the window open is dangerous as well since the dog can hurt himself trying to get out.

Make sure your dog is properly identified and that your contact information appears on his ID tags and on his crate. Animals travel in a different area of the plane than human passengers so every rule must be strictly adhered to so as to prevent the risk of getting separated from your dog.

BOARDING
So you want to take a family holiday—and you want to include all members of the family. You would probably make arrangements for accommodations ahead of time anyway, but this is especially important when travelling with a dog. You do not want to make an overnight stop at the only place around for miles and find out that they do not allow dogs. Also, you do not want to

TRAVEL TIP

For international travel you will have to make arrangements well in advance (perhaps months), as countries' regulations pertaining to bringing in animals differ. There may be special health certificates and/or vaccinations that your dog will need before taking the trip, sometimes this has to be done within a certain time frame. In rabies-free countries, you will need to bring proof of the dog's rabies vaccination and there may be a quarantine period upon arrival.

reserve a place for your family without confirming that you are travelling with a dog because if it is against their policy you may not have a place to stay.

Alternatively, if you are travelling and choose not to bring your Shih Tzu, you will have to make arrangements for him whilst you are away. Some options are to take him to a neighbour's house to stay whilst you are gone, to have a trusted neighbour stop by often or stay at your house, or bring your dog to a reputable boarding kennel. If you choose to board him at a kennel, you should visit in advance to see the facility, how clean they are and where the dogs are kept. Talk to some of the employees and see how they treat the dogs—have they experience in grooming long-coated dogs, do they spend time with the dogs, play with them, exercise them, etc.? Also find out the kennel's policy on vaccinations and what they require. This is for all of the

dogs' safety, since when dogs are kept together, there is a greater risk of diseases being passed from dog to dog.

IDENTIFICATION
Your Shih Tzu is your valued companion and friend. That is why you always keep a close eye on him and you have made sure that he cannot escape from the garden or wriggle out of his collar and run away from you. However, accidents can happen and there may come a time when your dog unexpectedly gets separated from you. If this unfortunate event should occur, the first thing on your mind will be finding him.

DID YOU KNOW?
The most extensive travel you do with your dog may be limited to trips to the veterinary surgeon's office—or you may decide to bring him along for long distances when the family goes on holiday. Whichever the case, it is important to consider your dog's safety while travelling.

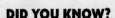

Proper identification, including an ID tag, a tattoo, and possibly a microchip, will increase the chances of his being returned to you safely and quickly.

DID YOU KNOW?
As puppies become more and more expensive, especially those puppies of high quality for showing and/or breeding, they have a greater chance of being stolen. The usual collar dog tag is, of course, easily removed. But there are two techniques that have become widely utilised for identification.

The puppy microchip implantation involves the injection of a small microchip, about the size of a corn kernel, under the skin of the dog. If your dog shows up at a clinic or shelter, or is offered for resale under less than savory circumstances, it can be positively identified by the microchip. The microchip is scanned and a registry quickly identifies you as the owner. This is not only protection against theft, but should the dog run away or go chasing a squirrel and get lost, you have a fair chance of getting it back.

Tattooing is done on various parts of the dog, from its belly to its cheeks. The number tattooed can be your telephone number or any other number which you can easily memorise. When professional dog thieves see a tattooed dog, they usually lose interest in it. Both microchipping and tattooing can be done at your local veterinary clinic. For the safety of our dogs, no laboratory facility or dog broker will accept a tattooed dog as stock.

Should you decide not to take your Shih Tzu on holiday with you, select a boarding facility that is well kept and run by exceptionally nice dog people.

Proper identification tags are a simple way to ensure that you will be able to retrieve your dog, should he wander away from home.

Shih Tzu

Living with an untrained dog is a lot like owning a piano that you do not know how to play—it is a nice object to look at but it does not do much more than that to bring you pleasure. Now try taking piano lessons and suddenly the piano comes alive and brings forth magical sounds and rhythms that set your heart singing and your body swaying.

The same is true with your Shih Tzu. Any dog is a big responsibility and if not trained sensibly may develop unacceptable behaviour that annoys you or could even cause family friction.

PATIENCE...

If you start with a normal, healthy dog and give him time, patience and some carefully executed lessons, you will reap the rewards of that training for the life of the dog. And what a life it will be! The two of you will find immeasurable pleasure in the companionship you have built together with love, respect and understanding. Good luck and enjoy!

To train your Shih Tzu, you may like to enrol in an obedience class. Teach him good manners as you learn how and why he behaves the way he does. Find out how to communicate with your dog and how to recognise and understand his communications with you. Suddenly the dog takes on a new role in your life—he is smart, interesting, well behaved and fun to be with. He demonstrates his bond of devotion to you daily. In other words, your Shih Tzu does wonders for your ego because he constantly reminds you that you are not only his leader, you are his hero!

Those involved with teaching dog obedience and counselling owners about their dogs' behaviour have discovered some interesting facts about dog ownership. For example, training dogs when they are puppies results in the highest rate of success in developing well-mannered and well-adjusted adult dogs. Training an older dog, from six months to six years of age, can produce almost equal results providing that the owner accepts the dog's slower rate of learning capability and is willing to work

DID YOU KNOW?

To a dog's way of thinking, your hands are like his mouth in terms of a defence mechanism. If you squeeze him too tightly, he might just bite you because that would be his normal response. This is not aggressive biting and, although all biting should be discouraged, you need to learn how to handle your dog.

patiently to help the dog succeed at developing to his fullest potential. Unfortunately, many owners of untrained adult dogs lack the patience factor, so they do not persist until their dogs are successful at learning particular behaviours.

Training a puppy, aged 10 to 16 weeks (20 weeks at the most) is like working with a dry sponge in a pool of water. The pup soaks up whatever you show him and constantly looks for more things to do and learn. At this early age, his body is not yet producing hormones, and therein lies the reason for such a high rate of success. Without hormones, he is focused on his owners and not particularly interested in investigating other places, dogs, people, etc. You are his leader: his provider of food, water, shelter and security. He latches onto you and wants to stay close. He will

usually follow you from room to room, will not let you out of his sight when you are outdoors with him, and respond in like manner to the people and animals you encounter. If you greet a friend warmly, he will be happy to greet the person as well. If, however, you are hesitant, even anxious, about the approach of a stranger, he will respond accordingly.

Once the puppy begins to produce hormones, his natural curiosity emerges and he begins to investigate the world around him. It is at this time when you may notice that the untrained dog begins to wander away from you and even ignore your commands to stay close.

There are usually classes within a reasonable distance of the owner's home, but you can also do a lot to train

DID YOU KNOW?

Training a dog is a life experience. Many parents admit that much of what they know about raising children they learned from caring for their dogs. Dogs respond to love, fairness and guidance, just as children do. Become a good dog owner and you may become an even better parent.

your dog yourself. Sometimes there are classes available but the tuition is too costly. Whatever the circumstances, the solution to the

Male dogs have a strong desire to mark their territory through urination. Females generally are easier to housebreak than males, since males tend to worry more about where to relieve themselves.

problem of lack of lesson availability lies within the pages of this book.

This chapter is devoted to helping you train your Shih Tzu at home. If the recommended procedures are followed faithfully, you may expect positive results

TRAINING TIP
Dogs are sensitive to their master's moods and emotions. Use your voice wisely when communicating with your dog. Never raise your voice at your dog unless you are angry and trying to correct him. 'Barking' at your dog can become as meaningless as 'dogspeak' is to you. Think before you bark!

MEALTIME...
Mealtime should be a peaceful time for your puppy. Do not put his food and water bowls in a high-traffic area in the house. For example, give him his own little corner of the kitchen where he can eat undisturbed and where he will not be under foot. Do not allow small children or other family members to disrupt the pup when he is eating.

that will prove rewarding to both you and your dog.

Whether your new charge is a puppy or a mature adult, the methods of teaching and the techniques we use in training basic behaviours are the same. After all, no dog, whether puppy or adult, likes harsh or inhumane methods. All creatures, however, respond favourably to gentle motivational methods and sincere praise and encouragement. Now let us get started.

HOUSEBREAKING
You can train a puppy to relieve itself wherever you choose, but this must be somewhere suitable. You should bear in mind from the outset that when your puppy is old enough to go out in public places, any canine deposits must be removed at once. You will always have to carry with you a small plastic bag or 'poop-scoop.'

DID YOU KNOW?
Dogs will do anything for your attention. If you reward the dog when he is calm and resting, you will develop a well-mannered dog. If, on the other hand, you greet your dog excitedly and encourage him to wrestle and roughhouse with you, the dog will greet you the same way and you will have a hyper dog on your hands.

Outdoor training includes such surfaces as grass, dirt and cement. Indoor training usually means training your dog to newspaper.

When deciding on the surface and location that you will want your Shih Tzu to use, be sure it is going to be permanent. Training your dog to grass and then changing your mind two months later is extremely difficult for both dog and owner.

Next, choose the command you will use each and every time you want your puppy to void. 'Go hurry up' and 'Toilet' are examples of commands commonly used by dog owners.

Get in the habit of giving the puppy your chosen relief command before you take him out. That way, when he becomes an adult, you will be able to determine if he wants to go out when you ask him. A confirma-tion will be signs of interest, wagging his tail, watching you intently, going to the door, etc.

PUPPY'S NEEDS
Puppy needs to relieve himself after play periods, after each meal, after he has been sleeping and any time he indicates that he is looking for a place to urinate or defecate.

The urinary and intestinal tract muscles of very young puppies are not fully developed. Therefore, like human babies, puppies need to relieve themselves frequently.

Take your puppy out often— every hour for an eight-week-old, for example, and always immediately after sleeping and eating. The older the puppy, the less often he will need to relieve himself.

DID YOU KNOW?
Dogs are the most honourable animals in existence. They consider another species (humans) as their own. They interface with you. You are their leader. Puppies perceive children to be on their level: their actions around small children are different than their behaviour around their adult masters.

Finally, as a mature healthy adult, he will require only three to five relief trips per day.

HOUSING

Since the types of housing and control you provide for your puppy have a direct relationship on the success of housetraining, we consider the various aspects of both before we begin training.

Bringing a new puppy home and turning him loose in your house can be compared to turning a child loose in a sports arena and telling the child that the place is all his! The sheer enormity of the place would be too much for him to handle.

Instead, offer the puppy clearly defined areas where he can play, sleep, eat and live. A room of the house where the

Dogs do not like to soil where they sleep. Let your puppy out often to relieve himself so he is not uncomfortable trying to 'hold it' in his crate.

DID YOU KNOW?
Your dog is actually training you at the same time you are training him. Dogs do things to get attention. They usually repeat whatever succeeds in getting your attention.

family gathers is the most obvious choice. Puppies are social animals and need to feel a part of the pack right from the start. Hearing your voice, watching you whilst you are

doing things and smelling you nearby are all positive reinforcers that he is now a member of your pack. Usually a family room, the kitchen or a nearby adjoining breakfast area is ideal for providing safety and security for both puppy and owner.

TRAINING TIP
Never line your pup's sleeping area with newspaper. Puppy litters are usually raised on newspaper and, once in your home, the puppy will immediately associate newspaper with voiding. Never put newspaper on any floor while housetraining, as this will only confuse the puppy. If you are paper-training him, use paper in his designated relief area ONLY. Finally, restrict water intake after evening meals. Offer a few licks at a time—never let a young puppy gulp water after meals.

Canine Development Schedule

It is important to understand how and at what age a puppy develops into adulthood. If you are a puppy owner, consult the following Canine Development Schedule to determine the stage of development your Shih Tzu puppy is currently experiencing. This knowledge will help you as you work with the puppy in the weeks and months ahead.

Period	Age	Characteristics
FIRST TO THIRD	BIRTH TO SEVEN WEEKS	Puppy needs food, sleep and warmth, and responds to simple and gentle touching. Needs mother for security and disciplining. Needs litter mates for learning and interacting with other dogs. Pup learns to function within a pack and learns pack order of dominance. Begin socialising with adults and children for short periods. Begins to become aware of its environment.
FOURTH	EIGHT TO TWELVE WEEKS	Brain is fully developed. Needs socialising with outside world. Remove from mother and littermates. Needs to change from canine pack to human pack. Human dominance necessary. Fear period occurs between 8 and 16 weeks. Avoid fright and pain.
FIFTH	THIRTEEN TO SIXTEEN WEEKS	Training and formal obedience should begin. Less association with other dogs, more with people, places, situations. Period will pass easily if you remember this is pup's change-to-adolescence time. Be firm and fair. Flight instinct prominent. Permissiveness and over-disciplining can do permanent damage. Praise for good behaviour.
JUVENILE	FOUR TO EIGHT MONTHS	Another fear period about 7 to 8 months of age. It passes quickly, but be cautious of fright and pain. Sexual maturity reached. Dominant traits established. Dog should understand sit, down, come and stay by now.

NOTE: THESE ARE APPROXIMATE TIME FRAMES. ALLOW FOR INDIVIDUAL DIFFERENCES IN PUPPIES.

Within that room there should be a smaller area which the puppy can call his own. An alcove, a wire or fibreglass dog crate or a fenced (not boarded!) corner from which he can view the activities

An open crate is fine for inside your home. For puppies, however, never put the water bowl inside the crate. This invites accidents when the puppy is crated.

of his new family will be fine. The size of the area or crate is the key factor here. The area must be large enough for the puppy to lie down and stretch out as well as stand up without rubbing his head on the top, yet small enough so that he cannot relieve himself at one end and sleep at the other without coming into contact with his droppings until fully trained to relieve himself outside.

TRAINING TIP

Stand up straight and authoritatively when giving your dog commands. Do not issue commands when lying on the floor or lying on your back on the sofa. If you are on your hands and knees when you give a command, your dog will think you are positioning yourself to play.

TRAINING TIP

The golden rule of dog training is simple. For each 'question' (command), there is only one correct answer (reaction). One command = one reaction. Keep practising the command until the dog reacts correctly without hesitating. Be repetitive but not monotonous. Dogs get bored just as people do!

Dogs are, by nature, clean animals and will not remain close to their relief areas unless forced to do so. In those cases, they then become dirty dogs and usually remain that way for life.

The designated area should be lined with clean bedding and a toy. Water must always be available, in a non-spill container.

CONTROL

By control, we mean helping the puppy to create a lifestyle pattern that will be compatible to that of his human pack (YOU!). Just as we guide little children to learn our way of life, we must show the puppy when it is time to play, eat, sleep, exercise and even entertain himself.

Your puppy should always sleep in his crate. He should also learn that, during times of household confusion and excessive human activity such as at breakfast when family

> **TRAINING TIP**
>
> Do not carry your dog to his toilet area. Lead him there on a leash or, better yet, encourage him to follow you to the spot. If you start carrying him to his spot, you might end up doing this routine forever and your dog will have the satisfaction of having trained YOU.

members are preparing for the day, he can play by himself in relative safety and comfort in his designated area. Each time you leave the puppy alone, he should understand exactly where he is to stay. You can gradually increase the time he is left alone to get him used to it. Puppies are chewers. They cannot tell the difference between lamp cords, television wires, shoes, table legs, etc. Chewing into a television wire, for example, can be fatal to the puppy whilst a shorted wire can start a fire in the house.

If the puppy chews on the arm of the chair when he is alone, you will probably discipline him angrily when you get home. Thus, he makes the association that your coming home means he is going to be punished. (He will not remember chewing up the chair and is incapable of making the association of the discipline with his naughty deed.)

Other times of excitement, such as family parties, etc., can be fun for the puppy providing he can view the activities from the security of his designated area. He is not underfoot and he is not being fed all sorts of titbits that will probably cause him stomach distress, yet he still feels a part of the fun.

SCHEDULE

A puppy should be taken to his relief area each time he is released from his designated area, after meals, after a play session, when he first awakens in the morning (at age eight weeks, this can mean 5 a.m.!). The puppy will indicate

> **TRAINING TIP**
>
> Practice Makes Perfect!
> • Have training lessons with your dog every day in several short segments— three to five times a day for a few minutes at a time is ideal.
> • Do not have long practice sessions. The dog will become easily bored.
> • Never practice when you are tired, ill, worried or in an otherwise negative mood. This will transmit to the dog and may have an adverse effect on its performance.
>
> Think fun, short and above all POSITIVE! End each session on a high note, rather than a failed exercise, and make sure to give a lot of praise. Enjoy the training and help your dog enjoy it, too.

that he's ready 'to go' by circling or sniffing busily—do not misinterpret these signs. For a puppy less than ten weeks of age, a routine of taking him out every hour is necessary. As the puppy grows, he will be able to wait for longer periods of time.

Keep trips to his relief area short. Stay no more than five or six minutes and then return to the house. If he goes during that time, praise him lavishly and take him indoors immediately. If he does not, but he has an accident when you go back indoors, pick him up immediately, say

THE SUCCESS METHOD

Success that comes by luck is usually short lived. Success that comes by well-thought-out proven methods is often more easily achieved and permanent. This is the Success Method. It is designed to give you, the puppy owner, a simple yet proven way to help your puppy develop clean living habits and a feeling of security in his new environment.

THE SUCCESS METHOD
6 Steps to Successful Crate Training

1 Tell the puppy 'Crate time!' and place him in the crate with a small treat (a piece of cheese or half of a biscuit). Let him stay in the crate for five minutes while you are in the same room. Then release him and praise lavishly. Never release him when he is fussing. Wait until he is quiet before you let him out.

2 Repeat Step 1 several times a day.

3 The next day, place the puppy in the crate as before. Let him stay there for ten minutes. Do this several times.

4 Continue building time in five-minute increments until the puppy

stays in his crate for 30 minutes with you in the room. Always take him to his relief area after prolonged periods in his crate.

5 Now go back to Step 1 and let the puppy stay in his crate for five minutes, this time while you are out of the room.

6 Once again, build crate time in five-minute increments with you out of the room. When the puppy will stay willingly in his crate (he may even fall asleep!) for 30 minutes with you out of the room, he will be ready to stay in it for several hours at a time.

HOW MANY TIMES A DAY?

AGE	RELIEF TRIPS
To 14 weeks	10
14–22 weeks	8
22–32 weeks	6
Adulthood	4
(dog stops growing)	

These are estimates, of course, but they are a guide to the MINIMUM opportunities a dog should have each day to relieve itself.

Help him develop regular hours for naps, being alone, playing by himself and just resting, all in his crate. Encourage him to

Always clean up after your dog, whether you're in a public place or your own garden.

entertain himself whilst you are busy with your activities. Let him learn that having you near is comforting, but it is not your main purpose in life to provide him with undivided attention.

Each time you put a puppy in his own area, use the same command, whatever suits best. Soon, he will run to his crate or

'No! No!' and return to his relief area. Wait a few minutes, then return to the house again. never hit a puppy or rub his face in urine or excrement when he has an accident!

Once indoors, put the puppy in his crate until you have had time to clean up his accident. Then release him to the family area and watch him more closely than before. Chances are, his accident was a result of your not picking up his signal or waiting too long before offering him the opportunity to relieve himself. Never hold a grudge against the puppy for accidents.

Let the puppy learn that going outdoors means it is time to relieve himself, not play. Once trained, he will be able to play indoors and out and still differentiate between the times for play versus the times for relief.

TRAINING TIP

By providing sleeping and resting quarters that fit the dog, and offering frequent opportunities to relieve himself outside his quarters, the puppy quickly learns that the outdoors (or the newspaper if you are training him to paper) is the place to go when he needs to urinate or defecate. It also reinforces his innate desire to keep his sleeping quarters clean. This, in turn, helps develop the muscle control that will eventually produce a dog with clean living habits.

TRAINING TIP

If you want to be successful in training your dog, you have four rules to obey yourself:
1. Develop an understanding of how a dog thinks.
2. Do not blame the dog for lack of communication.
3. Define your dog's personality and act accordingly.
4. Have patience and be consistent.

When performing brings forth happy rewards, the Shih Tzu will readily repeat the behaviour. Shih Tzu can be trained to do almost anything!

special area when he hears you say those words.

Crate training provides safety for you, the puppy and the home. It also provides the puppy with a feeling of security, and that helps the puppy achieve self-confidence and clean habits.

Remember that one of the primary ingredients in housetrain-ing your puppy is control. Regardless of your lifestyle, there will always be occasions when you will need to have a place where your dog can stay and be happy and safe. Training is the answer for now and in the future.

In conclusion, a few key elements are really all you need for a successful house training method—consistency, frequency, praise, control and supervision. By following these procedures with a normal, healthy puppy, you and the puppy will soon be past the stage of 'accidents' and ready to move on to a full and rewarding life together.

ROLES OF DISCIPLINE, REWARD AND PUNISHMENT

Discipline, training one to act in accordance with rules, brings order to life. It is as simple as that. Without discipline, particularly in a group society, chaos

DID YOU KNOW?

The puppy should also have regular play and exercise sessions when he is with you or a family member. Exercise for a very young puppy can consist of a short walk around the house or garden. Playing can include fetching games with a large ball or a special raggy. (All puppies teethe and need soft things upon which to chew.) Remember to restrict play periods to indoors within his living area (the family room for example) until he is completely housetrained.

TRAINING TIP

Never train your dog, puppy or adult, when you are mad or in a sour mood. Dogs are very sensitive to human feelings, especially anger, and if your dog senses that you are angry or upset, he will connect your anger with his training and learn to resent or fear his training sessions.

reigns supreme and the group will eventually perish. Humans and canines are social animals and need some form of discipline in order to function effectively. They must procure food, protect their home base and their young and reproduce to keep the species going.

If there were no discipline in the lives of social animals, they would eventually die from starvation and/or predation by other stronger animals.

In the case of domestic canines, dogs need discipline in their lives in order to understand how their pack (you and other family members) functions and how they must act in order to survive.

A large humane society in a highly populated area recently surveyed dog owners regarding their satisfaction with their relationships with their dogs. People who had trained their dogs were 75% more satisfied with their pets than those who had never trained their dogs.

Dr Edward Thorndike, a psychologist, established *Thorndike's Theory of Learning*, which states that a behaviour that results in a pleasant event tends

A puppy is perhaps the most impression-able creature on the planet. You mould your puppy to become the companion you want him to be.

DID YOU KNOW?

Dogs do not understand our language. They can be trained to react to a certain sound, at a certain volume. If you say 'No, Oliver' in a very soft pleasant voice it will not have the same meaning as 'No, Oliver!!' when you shout it as loud as you can. You should never use the dog's name during a reprimand, just the command NO!! Since dogs don't understand words, comics use dogs trained with opposite meanings. Thus, when the comic commands his dog to SIT the dog will stand up; and vice versa.

to be repeated. A behaviour that results in an unpleasant event tends not to be repeated. It is this theory on which training methods are based today. For example, if you manipulate a dog to perform a specific behaviour and reward him for doing it, he is likely to do it again because he enjoyed the end result.

Good performances during training should be rewarded with a treat. Treats really inspire dogs to perform.

Occasionally, punishment, a penalty inflicted for an offence, is necessary. The best type of punishment often comes from an outside source. For example, a child is told not to touch the stove because he may get burned. He disobeys and touches the stove. In doing so, he receives a burn. From that time on, he respects the heat of the stove and avoids contact with it. Therefore, a behaviour that results in an unpleasant event tends not to be repeated.

A good example of a dog learning the hard way is the dog who chases the house cat. He is told many times to leave the cat alone, yet he persists in teasing the cat. Then, one day he begins chasing the cat but the cat turns and swipes a claw across the dog's face, leaving him with a painful gash on his nose. The final result is that the dog stops chasing the cat.

TRAINING EQUIPMENT
COLLAR AND LEAD
For a Shih Tzu the collar and lead that you use for training must be one with which you are easily able to work, not too heavy for the dog and perfectly safe.

TREATS
Have a bag of treats on hand. Something nutritious and easy to swallow works best. Use a soft treat, a chunk of cheese or a piece of cooked chicken rather than a dry biscuit. By the time the dog gets done chewing a dry treat, he will forget why he is being rewarded in the first place! Using food rewards will not teach a dog to beg at the table—the only way to teach a dog to beg at the table is to give him food from the table. In

---

TRAINING TIP
Dogs are as different from each other as people are. What works for one dog may not work for another. Have an open mind. If one method of training is unsuccessful, try another.

---

training, rewarding the dog with a food treat will help him associate praise and the treats with learning new behaviours that obviously please his owner.

TRAINING BEGINS: ASK THE DOG A QUESTION

In order to teach your dog anything, you must first get his attention. After all, he cannot learn anything if he is looking away from you with his mind on something else.

To get his attention, ask him, 'School?' and immediately walk over to him and give him a treat as you tell him 'Good dog.' Wait a minute or two and repeat the routine, this time with a treat in

'Good dog! Good sit!' Teaching the sit is the beginning of your Shih Tzu's education.

your hand as you approach within a foot of the dog. Do not directly to him, but stop about a foot short of him and hold out the treat as you ask, 'School?' He will see you approaching with a treat in your hand and most likely begin walking toward you. As you meet, give him the treat and praise again.

The third time, ask the question, have a treat in your hand and walk only a short distance toward the dog so that he must walk almost all the way to you. As he reaches you, give him the treat and praise again.

By this time, the dog will probably be getting the idea that if he pays attention to you, especially when you ask that question, it will pay off in treats and fun

It is better to use a soft treat, in small pieces, to reward your Shih Tzu. Cheese or a freeze-dried liver is an ideal treat.

activities for him. In other words, he learns that 'school' means doing fun things with you that result in treats and positive attention for him.

As the down position is one of submission to a dog, teaching your Shih Tzu the down position can be very frustrating for the owner and dog alike.

Remember that the dog does not understand your verbal language, he only recognises sounds. Your question translates to a series of sounds for him, and those sounds become the signal to go to you and pay attention; if he does, he will get to interact with you plus receive treats and praise.

THE BASIC COMMANDS
TEACHING SIT
Now that you have the dog's attention, attach his lead and hold it in your left hand and a food treat in your right. Place your food hand at the dog's nose and let him lick the treat but not take it from you. Say 'Sit' and slowly raise

your food hand from in front of the dog's nose up over his head so that he is looking at the ceiling. As he bends his head upward, he will have to bend his knees to maintain his balance. As he bends his knees, he will assume a sit position. At that point, release the food treat and praise lavishly with comments such as 'Good dog! Good sit!', etc. Remember to always praise enthusiastically, because dogs relish verbal praise from their owners and feel so proud of themselves whenever they accomplish a behaviour.

You will not use food forever in getting the dog to obey your commands. Food is only used to teach new behaviours, and once the dog knows what you want when you give a specific command, you will wean him off of the food treats but still maintain the verbal praise. After all, you will always have your voice with you, and there will be many times when you have no

> **DID YOU KNOW?**
> A dog in jeopardy never lies down. He stays alert on his feet because instinct tells him that he may have to run away or fight for his survival. Therefore, if a dog feels threatened or anxious, he will not lie down. Consequently, it is important to have the dog calm and relaxed as he learns the down exercise.

food rewards but expect the dog to obey.

TEACHING DOWN

Teaching the down exercise is easy when you understand how the dog perceives the down position, and it is very difficult when you do not. Dogs perceive the down position as a submissive one, therefore teaching the down exercise using a forceful method can sometimes make the dog

Teaching to stay begins either in the sitting or down position.

You can use a treat to enhance your dog's desire to learn, but eventually the dog must be weaned off the food reward.

develop such a fear of the down that he either runs away when you say 'Down' or he attempts to snap at the person who tries to force him down.

Have the dog sit close alongside your left leg, facing in the same direction as you are. Hold the lead in your left hand and a food treat in your right. Now place your left hand lightly on the top of the dog's shoulders where they meet above the spinal cord. Do not push down on the dog's shoulders; simply rest your left hand there so you can guide the dog to lie down close to your left leg rather than to swing away from your side when he drops.

Now place the food hand at the dog's nose, say 'Down' very softly (almost a whisper), and slowly lower the food hand to the dog's front feet. When the food hand reaches the floor, begin moving it forward along the floor in front of the dog. Keep talking softly to the dog, saying things like, 'Do you want this treat? You can do this, good dog.' Your reassuring tone of voice will help calm the dog as he tries to follow the food hand in order to get the treat.

101

Your Shih Tzu will be anxious to please you. Stay is amongst the easiest commands as your dog does not have to exert much effort to receive rewards and praise.

When the dog's elbows touch the floor, release the food and praise softly. Try to get the dog to maintain that down position for several seconds before you let him sit up again. The goal here is to get the dog to settle down and not feel threatened in the down position.

TEACHING STAY

It is easy to teach the dog to stay in either a sit or a down position. Again, we use food and praise during the teaching process as we help the dog to understand exactly what it is that we are expecting him to do.

To teach the sit/stay, start with the dog sitting on your left side as before and hold the lead in your left hand. Have a food treat in your right hand and place your food hand at the dog's nose. Say 'Stay' and step out on your right foot to stand directly in front of the dog, toe to toe, as he licks and nibbles the treat. Be sure to keep

TRAINING TIP

When calling the dog, do not say 'Come.' Say things like, 'Rover, where are you? See if you can find me! I have a cookie for you!' Keep up a constant line of chatter with coaxing sounds and frequent questions such as, 'Where are you?' The dog will learn to follow the sound of your voice to locate you and receive his reward.

his head facing upward to maintain the sit position. Count to five and then swing around to stand next to the dog again with him on your left. As soon as you get back to the original position, release the food and praise lavishly.

To teach the down/stay, do the down as previously described. As soon as the dog lies down, say 'Stay' and step out on your right foot just as you did in the sit/stay. Count to five and then return to stand beside the dog with him on your left side. Release the treat and praise as always.

Within a week or ten days, you can begin to add a bit of distance between you and your dog when you leave him. When you do, use your left hand open with the palm facing the dog as a stay signal, much the same as the hand signal a police officer uses to stop traffic at an intersection. Hold the food treat in your right

hand as before, but this time the food is not touching the dog's nose. He will watch the food hand and quickly learn that he is going to get that treat as soon as you return to his side.

When you can stand 1 metre away from your dog for 30 seconds, you can then begin building time and distance in both stays. Eventually, the dog can be expected to remain in the stay position for prolonged periods of time until you return to him or call him to you. Always praise lavishly when he stays.

Your rapport with your Shih Tzu is a major factor in teaching the come. Your dog must be anxious to find you and to be near you.

TEACHING COME

If you make teaching 'come' a fun experience, you should never have a 'student' that does not love the game or that fails to come when called. The secret, it seems, is never to teach the word 'come.'

At times when an owner most wants his dog to come when

TRAINING TIP

Never call your dog to come to you for a correction or scold him when he reaches you. That is the quickest way to turn a 'Come' command into 'Go away fast!' Dogs think only in the present tense and he will connect the scolding with coming to his master, not with the misbehaviour of a few moments earlier.

called, the owner is likely upset or anxious and he allows these feelings to come through in the tone of his voice when he calls his dog. Hearing that desperation in his owner's voice, the dog fears the results of going to him and therefore either disobeys outright or runs in the opposite direction. The secret, therefore, is to teach the dog a game and, when you want him to come to you, simply play the game. It is practically a no-fail solution!

To begin, have several members of your family take a few food treats and each go into a different room in the house. Take

TRAINING TIP
Play fetch games with your puppy in an enclosed area where he can retrieve his toy and bring

it back to you. Always use a toy or object designated just for this purpose. Never use a shoe, sock or other item he may later confuse with those in your closet or underneath your chair.

TRAINING TIP
If you begin teaching the heel by taking long walks and letting the dog pull you along, he misinterprets this action as an acceptable form of taking a walk. When you pull back on the lead to counteract his pulling, he reads that tug as a signal to pull even harder!

turns calling the dog, and each person should celebrate the dog's finding him with a treat and lots of happy praise. When a person calls the dog, he is actually inviting the dog to find him and get a treat as a reward for 'winning.'

A few turns of the 'Where are you?' game and the dog will figure out that everyone is playing the game and that each person has a big celebration awaiting his success at locating them. Once he learns to love the game, simply calling out 'Where are you?' will bring him running from wherever he is when he hears that all-important question.

The come command is recognised as one of the most important things to teach a dog, but there are trainers who work with thousands of dogs and never teach the actual word 'Come.' Yet these dogs will race to respond to a person who uses the dog's name followed by 'Where are you?' For example, a woman has a 12-year-

patience on the owner's part to succeed at teaching the dog that he (the owner) will not proceed unless the dog is walking calmly beside him. Pulling out ahead on the lead is definitely not acceptable.

Begin with holding the lead in your left hand as the dog sits beside your left leg. Move the loop end of the lead to your right hand but keep your left hand short on the lead so it keeps the dog in close next to you.

Say 'Heel' and step forward on your left foot. Keep the dog close to you and take three steps. Stop and have the dog sit next to you in what we now call the 'heel position.' Praise verbally, but do not touch the dog. Hesitate a moment and begin again with 'Heel,' taking three steps and stopping, at which

Do not attempt to teach your dog more than one command in any given lesson. Keep training sessions short and sweet or you will lose your dog's attention.

old companion dog who went blind, but who never fails to locate her owner when asked, 'Where are you?'

Children particularly love to play this game with their dogs. Children can hide in smaller places like a shower or bathtub, behind a bed or under a table. The dog needs to work a little bit harder to find these hiding places, but when he does he loves to celebrate with a treat and a tussle with a favourite youngster.

TEACHING HEEL
Heeling means that the dog walks beside the owner without pulling. It takes time and

---

TRAINING TIP
Teach your dog to HEEL in an enclosed area. Once you think the dog will obey reliably and you want to attempt advanced obedience exercises such as off-lead heeling, test him in a fenced in area so he cannot run away.

---

point the dog is told to sit again.

Your goal here is to have the dog walk those three steps without pulling on the lead. When he will walk calmly beside

Successful heel training is the basis of walking on a lead. Work diligently on the heel lesson and you will be rewarded with a dog who is a joy to walk his whole life.

want him to heel. When you stop heeling, indicate to the dog that the exercise is over by verbally praising as you pet him and say 'OK, good dog.' The 'OK' is used as a release word meaning that the exercise is finished and the dog is free to relax.

If you are dealing with a dog who insists on pulling you around, simply 'put on your brakes' and stand your ground until the dog realises that the two of you are not going anywhere until he is beside you and moving at your pace, not his. It may take some time just standing there to convince the dog that you are the leader and you will be the one to decide on the direction and speed of your travel.

you for three steps without pulling, increase the number of steps you take to five. When he will walk politely beside you whilst you take five steps, you can increase the length of your walk to ten steps. Keep increasing the length of your stroll until the dog will walk quietly beside you without pulling as long as you

Each time the dog looks up at you or slows down to give a slack lead between the two of you, quietly praise him and say, 'Good heel. Good dog.' Eventually, the dog will begin to respond and

TRAINING TIP
If you are walking your dog and he suddenly stops and looks straight into your eyes, ignore him. Pull the leash and lead him into the direction you want to walk.

understands what behaviour goes with a specific command, it is time to start weaning him off the food treats. At first, give a treat after each exercise. Then, start to give a treat only after every other exercise. Mix up the times when you offer a food reward and the times when you only offer praise so that the dog will never know

This Shih Tzu is manoeuvring the pipe and collapsed tunnels at an agility trial.

within a few days he will be walking politely beside you without pulling on the lead. At first, the training sessions should be kept short and very positive; soon the dog will be able to walk

nicely with you for increasingly longer distances. Remember also to give the dog free time and the opportunity to run and play when you are done with heel practice.

WEANING OFF FOOD IN TRAINING
Food is used in training new behaviours. Once the dog

Weave poles are a popular obstacle at agility trials. Shih Tzu can be trained to tackle most agility obstacles with grace and enthusiasm.

when he is going to receive both food and praise and when he is going to receive only praise. This is called a variable ratio reward system and it proves successful because there is always the chance that the owner will produce a treat, so the dog never stops trying for that reward. No matter what, ALWAYS give verbal praise.

OBEDIENCE CLASSES

It is a good idea to enrol in an obedience class if one is available in your area. If yours is a show dog, ringcraft classes would be more appropriate. Many areas have dog clubs that offer basic obedience training as well as preparatory classes for obedience competition. There are also local dog trainers who offer similar classes.

At obedience trials, dogs can earn titles at various levels of competition. The beginning levels of competition include basic behaviours such as sit, down, heel, etc. The more

advanced levels of competition include jumping, retrieving, scent discrimination and signal work. The advanced levels require a dog and owner to put a lot of time and effort into their training and the titles that can be earned at these levels of competition are very prestigious.

DID YOU KNOW?
Taking your dog to an obedience school may be the best investment in time and money you can ever make. You will enjoy the benefits for the lifetime of your dog and you will have the opportunity to meet people with similar expectations for companion dogs.

OTHER ACTIVITIES FOR LIFE

Whether a dog is trained in the structured environment of a class or alone with his owner at home, there are many activities that can bring fun and rewards to both owner and dog once they have mastered basic control.

Teaching the dog to help out around the home, in the garden or on the farm provides great satisfaction to both dog and

The Shih Tzu is a very focused competitor. He is very intelligent and can remember the obstacle course. What he lacks in leg, he makes up in brains.

owner. In addition, the dog's help makes life a little easier for his owner and raises his stature as a valued companion to his family. It helps give the dog a purpose by occupying his mind and providing an outlet for his energy.

Backpacking is an exciting and healthy activity that the dog can be taught without assistance from more than his owner. The exercise of walking and climbing is good for man and dog alike, and the bond that they develop together is priceless.

Shih Tzu are natural jumpers—whether it's the long jump or the high jump. Of course, agility trials adjust the measurements for the diminutive Shih Tzu.

Small dogs, like Shih Tzu, have a size advantage in the tunnel. They usually are more successful than larger dogs that can't stand up in the tunnel.

Internal Structure of the Shih Tzu

1. Esophagus
2. Lungs
3. Gall Bladder
4. Liver
5. Kidney
6. Stomach
7. Intestines
8. Urinary Bladder

Shih Tzu

Dogs suffer many of the same physical illnesses as people. They might even share many of the same psychological problems. Since people usually know more about human diseases than canine maladies, many of the terms used in this chapter will be familiar but not necessarily those used by veterinary surgeons. We will use the term x-ray, instead of the more acceptable term radiograph. We will also use the familiar term symptoms even though dogs don't have symptoms, which are verbal descriptions of the patient's feelings: dogs have clinical signs. Since dogs can't speak, we have to look for clinical signs...but we still use the term symptoms in this book.

As a general rule, medicine is practised. That term is not arbitrary. Medicine is a constantly changing art as we learn more and more about genetics, electronic aids (like CAT scans) and daily laboratory advances. There are many dog maladies, like canine hip dysplasia, which are not universally treated in the same manner. Some veterinary surgeons opt for surgery more often than others do.

SELECTING A VETERINARY SURGEON

Your selection of a veterinary surgeon should not be based upon personality (as most are) but upon their convenience to your home. You want a doctor who is close because you might have emergencies or need to make multiple visits for treatments. You want a doctor who has services that you might require such as a boarding kennel and grooming facilities, as well as sophisticated pet supplies and a good reputation for ability and responsiveness. There is nothing more frustrating than having to wait a day or more to get a response from your veterinary surgeon.

Before you buy your Shih Tzu, meet and interview the veterinary surgeons in your area. Take everything into consideration; discuss his background, specialities, fees, emergency policy, etc.

A typical American vet's income categorised according to services performed. This survey dealt with small-animal (pets) practices.

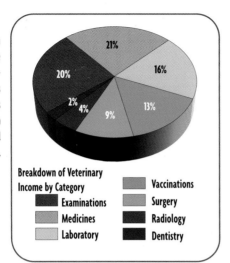

Breakdown of Veterinary Income by Category

- Examinations
- Medicines
- Laboratory
- Vaccinations
- Surgery
- Radiology
- Dentistry

All veterinary surgeons are licensed and their diplomas and/or certificates should be displayed in their waiting rooms. There are, however, many veterinary specialties that usually require further studies and internships. There are specialists in heart problems (veterinary cardiologists), skin problems (veterinary dermatologists), teeth and gum problems (veterinary dentists), eye problems (veterinary ophthalmologists), X-rays (veterinary radiologists), and surgeons who have specialties in bones, muscles or other organs. Most veterinary surgeons do routine surgery such as neutering, stitching up wounds and docking tails for those breeds in which such is required for show purposes. When the problem affecting your dog is serious, it is not unusual or impudent to get another medical opinion, although in Britain you are obliged to advise the vets concerned about this. You might also want to compare costs amongst several veterinary surgeons. Sophisticated health care and veterinary services can be very costly. Don't be bashful about discussing these costs with your veterinary surgeon or his (her) staff. It is not infrequent that important decisions are based upon financial considerations.

PREVENTATIVE MEDICINE

It is much easier, less costly and more effective to practise preventative medicine than to fight bouts of illness and disease. Properly bred puppies come from parents that were selected based upon their genetic disease profile. Their mothers should have been vaccinated, free of all internal and external parasites, and properly nourished. For these reasons, a visit to the veterinary surgeon who cared for the dam (mother) is recommended. The dam can pass

DID YOU KNOW?

Male dogs are neutered. The operation removes the testicles and requires that the dog be anaesthetised. Recovery takes about one week. Females are spayed. This is major surgery and it usually takes a bitch two weeks to recover.

First Aid
at a Glance

Burns
Place the affected area under cool water; use ice if only a small area is burnt.

Bee/Insect bites
Apply ice to relieve swelling; antihistamine dosed properly.

Animal bites
Clean any bleeding area; apply pressure until bleeding subsides; go to the vet.

Spider bites
Use cold compress and a pressurised pack to inhibit venom's spreading.

Antifreeze poisoning
Immediately induce vomiting by using hydrogen peroxide.

Fish hooks
Removal best handled by vet; hook must be cut in order to remove.

Snake bites
Pack ice around bite; contact vet quickly; identify snake for proper antivenin.

Car accident
Move dog from roadway with blanket; seek veterinary aid.

Shock
Calm the dog, keep him warm; seek immediate veterinary help.

Nosebleed
Apply cold compress to the nose; apply pressure to any visible abrasion.

Bleeding
Apply pressure above the area; treat wound by applying a cotton pack.

Heat stroke
Submerge dog in cold bath; cool down with fresh air and water; go to the vet.

Frostbite/Hypothermia
Warm the dog with a warm bath, electric blankets or hot water bottles.

Abrasions
Clean the wound and wash out thoroughly with fresh water; apply antiseptic.

 Remember: an injured dog may attempt to bite a helping hand from fear and confusion. Always muzzle the dog before trying to offer assistance.

on disease resistance to her puppies, which can last for eight to ten weeks. She can also pass on parasites and many infections. That's why you should visit the veterinary surgeon who cared for the dam.

WEANING TO FIVE MONTHS OLD
Puppies should be weaned by the time they are about two months old. A puppy that remains for at least eight weeks with its mother and litter mates usually adapts better to other dogs and people later in its life.

Some new owners have their puppy examined by a veterinary surgeon immediately, which is a good idea. Vaccination programmes usually begin when the puppy is very young.

The puppy will have its teeth examined and have its skeletal conformation and general health checked prior to certification by the veterinary surgeon. Puppies in

> **DID YOU KNOW?**
> Cases of hyperactive adrenal glands (Cushing's disease) have been traced to the drinking of highly chlorinated water. Aerate or age your dog's drinking water before offering it.

certain breeds have problems with their kneecaps, eye cataracts and other eye problems, heart murmurs and undescended testicles. They may also have personality problems and your veterinary surgeon might have training in temperament evaluation.

VACCINATION SCHEDULING
Most vaccinations are given by injection and should only be done by a veterinary surgeon. Both he and you should keep a record of the date of the injection, the identification of the vaccine and the amount given. Some vets give a first vaccination at eight weeks, but most dog breeders prefer the course not to commence until about ten weeks because of negating any antibodies passed on by the dam. The vaccination scheduling is usually based on a 15-day cycle. You must take your vet's advice as to when to vaccinate as this may differ according to the vaccine used. Most vaccinations immunise your puppy against viruses.

The usual vaccines contain immunising doses of several

> **DID YOU KNOW?**
> Caring for the puppy starts before the puppy is born by keeping the dam healthy and well-nourished. Most puppies have worms, even if they are not evident, so a worming programme is essential. The worms continually shed eggs except during their dormant stage, when they just rest in the tissues of the puppy. During this stage they are not evident during a routine examination.

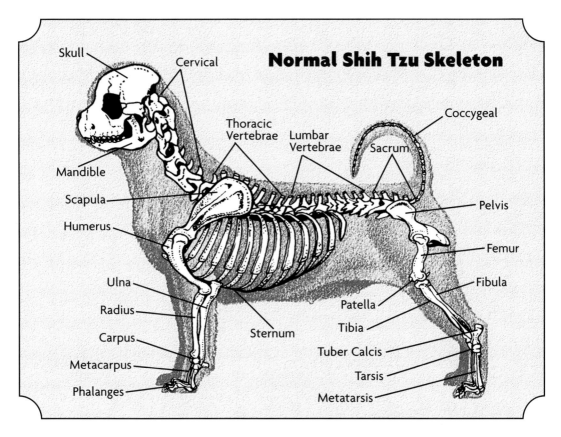

Normal Shih Tzu Skeleton

Skull
Cervical
Thoracic Vertebrae
Lumbar Vertebrae
Coccygeal
Sacrum
Mandible
Scapula
Pelvis
Humerus
Femur
Ulna
Fibula
Radius
Patella
Carpus
Tibia
Metacarpus
Sternum
Tuber Calcis
Phalanges
Tarsis
Metatarsis

different viruses such as distemper, parvovirus, parainfluenza and hepatitis. There are other vaccines available when the puppy is at risk. You should rely upon professional advice. This is especially true for the booster-shot programme. Most vaccination programmes require a booster when the puppy is a year old and once a year thereafter. In some cases, circumstances may require more frequent immunisations.

Kennel cough, more formally known as tracheobronchitis, is treated with a vaccine that is sprayed into the dog's nostrils.

Kennel cough is usually included in routine vaccination, but this is often not so effective as for other major diseases.

DID YOU KNOW?

Not every dog's ears are the same. Ears that are open to the air are healthier than ears with poor air circulation. Sometimes a dog can have two differently shaped ears. You should not probe inside your dog's ears. Only clean that which is accessible with a soft cotton wipe.

HEALTH AND VACCINATION SCHEDULE

Age in Weeks:	3rd	6th	8th	10th	12th	14th	16th	20-24th
Worm Control	✔	✔	✔	✔	✔	✔	✔	✔
Neutering								✔
Heartworm*		✔						✔
Parvovirus		✔		✔		✔		✔
Distemper			✔		✔		✔	
Hepatitis			✔		✔		✔	
Leptospirosis		✔		✔		✔		
Parainfluenza		✔		✔		✔		
Dental Examination			✔					✔
Complete Physical			✔					✔
Temperament Testing			✔					
Coronavirus					✔			
Kennel Cough		✔						
Hip Dysplasia							✔	
Rabies*								✔

Vaccinations are not instantly effective. It takes about two weeks for the dog's immunisation system to develop antibodies. Most vaccinations require annual booster shots. Your veterinary surgeon should guide you in this regard.
*Not applicable in the United Kingdom

FIVE MONTHS TO ONE YEAR OF AGE
Unless you intend to breed or show your dog, neutering the puppy at six months of age is recommended. Discuss this with your veterinary surgeon.

By the time your Shih Tzu is seven or eight months of age, he can be seriously evaluated for his conformation to the standard, thus determining show potential and desirability as a sire or dam. If the puppy is not top class and therefore is not a candidate for a serious breeding programme, most professionals advise neutering the puppy. Neutering has proven to be extremely beneficial to both male and female puppies. Besides eliminating the possibility of pregnancy, it inhibits (but does

DID YOU KNOW?
Vaccines do not work all the time. Sometimes dogs are allergic to them and many times the antibodies, which are supposed to be stimulated by the vaccine, just are not produced. You should keep your dog in the veterinary clinic for an hour after it is vaccinated to be sure there are no allergic reactions.

not prevent) breast cancer in bitches and prostate cancer in male dogs. Under no circumstances should a bitch be spayed prior to her first season.

DOGS OLDER THAN ONE YEAR

Continue to visit the veterinary surgeon at least once a year. There is no such disease as old age, but bodily functions do change with age. The eyes and ears are no longer as efficient. Liver, kidney and intestinal functions often decline. Proper dietary changes, recommended by your veterinary surgeon, can make life more pleasant for the ageing Shih Tzu and you.

DID YOU KNOW?
Your veterinary surgeon will probably recommend that your puppy be vaccinated before you take him outside. There are airborne diseases, parasite eggs in the grass and unexpected visits from other dogs that might be dangerous to your puppy's health.

SKIN PROBLEMS IN SHIH TZU

Veterinary surgeons are consulted by dog owners for skin problems more than any other group of diseases or maladies. Dogs' skin is almost as sensitive as human skin and both suffer almost the same

Disease	What is it?	What causes it?	Symptoms
Leptospirosis	Severe disease that affects the internal organs; can be spread to people.	A bacterium, which is often carried by rodents, that enters through mucous membranes and spreads quickly throughout the body.	Range from fever, vomiting and loss of appetite in less severe cases to shock, irreversible kidney damage and possibly death in most severe cases.
Rabies	Potentially deadly virus that infects warm-blooded mammals. Not seen in United Kingdom.	Bite from a carrier of the virus, mainly wild animals.	1st stage: dog exhibits change in behaviour, fear. 2nd stage: dog's behaviour becomes more aggressive. 3rd stage: loss of coordination, trouble with bodily functions.
Parvovirus	Highly contagious virus, potentially deadly.	Ingestion of the virus, which is usually spread through the faeces of infected dogs.	Most common: severe diarrhoea. Also vomiting, fatigue, lack of appetite.
Kennel cough	Contagious respiratory infection.	Combination of types of bacteria and virus. Most common: *Bordetella bronchiseptica* bacteria and parainfluenza virus.	Chronic cough.
Distemper	Disease primarily affecting respiratory and nervous system.	Virus that is related to the human measles virus.	Mild symptoms such as fever, lack of appetite and mucous secretion progress to evidence of brain damage, 'hard pad.'
Hepatitis	Virus primarily affecting the liver.	Canine adenovirus type I (CAV-1). Enters system when dog breathes in particles.	Lesser symptoms include listlessness, diarrhoea, vomiting. More severe symptoms include 'blue-eye' (clumps of virus in eye).
Coronavirus	Virus resulting in digestive problems.	Virus is spread through infected dog's faeces.	Stomach upset evidenced by lack of appetite, vomiting, diarrhoea.

A dental examination is in order when the dog is between six months and one year of age so any permanent teeth that have erupted incorrectly can be corrected. It is important to begin a brushing routine, preferably using a two-sided brushing technique, whereby both sides of the tooth are brushed at the same time. Durable nylon and safe edible chews should be a part of your puppy's arsenal for good health, good teeth and pleasant breath. The vast majority of dogs three to four years old and older has diseases of their gums from lack of dental attention. Using the various types of dental chews can be very effective in controlling dental plaque.

By the time your dog is a year old, you should have become very comfortable with your local veterinary surgeon and have agreed on scheduled visits for booster vaccinations. Blood tests should now be taken regularly, for comparative purposes, for such variables as cholesterol and triglyceride levels, thyroid hormones, liver enzymes, blood cell counts, etc.

The eyes, ears, nose and throat should be examined regularly and annual cleaning of the teeth is a ritual. For teeth scaling, the dog must be anaesthetised.

ailments. (Though the occurrence of acne in dogs is rare!) For this reason, veterinary dermatology has developed into a speciality practised by many veterinary surgeons.

Since many skin problems have visual symptoms that are almost identical, it requires the skill of an experienced veterinary dermatologist to identify and cure many of the more severe skin disorders. Pet shops sell many treatments for skin problems but most of the treatments are directed at symptoms and not the underlying problem(s). If your dog is suffering from a skin disorder, you should seek professional assistance as quickly as possible. As with all diseases, the earlier a problem is identified and treated, the more successful is the cure.

INHERITED SKIN PROBLEMS
Many skin disorders are inherited and some are fatal. For example, Acrodermatitis is an inherited disease that is transmitted by both parents. The parents, who appear (phenotypically) normal, have a recessive gene for acrodermatitis, meaning that they carry, but are not affected by the disease.

Acrodermatitis is just one example of how difficult it is to prevent congenital dog diseases. The cost and skills required to ascertain whether two dogs should be mated are too high even though puppies with acrodermatitis rarely reach two years of age.

Other inherited skin problems are usually not as fatal as acrodermatitis. All inherited diseases must be diagnosed and treated by a veterinary specialist. There are active programmes being undertaken by many veterinary pharmaceutical manufacturers to solve most, if not all, of the common skin problems of dogs.

PARASITE BITES

Many of us are allergic to insect bites. The bites itch, erupt and may even become infected. Dogs have the same reaction to fleas, ticks and/or mites. When an insect lands on you, you have the chance to whisk it away with your hand. Unfortunately, when our dog is bitten by a flea, tick or mite, it can only scratch it away or bite it. By the time the dog has been bitten, the parasite has done some of its damage. It may also have laid eggs to cause further problems in the near future. The itching from parasite bites is probably due to the saliva injected into the site when the parasite sucks the dog's blood.

ACRODERMATITIS

There is a 25% chance of a puppy getting this fatal gene combination from two parents with recessive genes for acrodermatitis:

AA= NORMAL, HEALTHY
aa= FATAL
Aa= RECESSIVE, NORMAL APPEARING

If the female parent has an Aa gene and the male parent has an Aa gene, the chances are one in four that the puppy will have the fatal genetic combination aa.

		Dam	
		A	a	♀
Sire	A	AA	Aa
	a	Aa	aa
	♂		

DID YOU KNOW?

Feeding your dog properly is very important. An incorrect diet could affect the dog's health, behaviour and nervous system, having a very significant effect on the dog's skin and coat.

AIRBORNE ALLERGIES

Another interesting allergy is pollen allergy. Humans have hay fever, rose fever and other fevers with which they suffer during the pollinating season. Many dogs suffer the same allergies. When the pollen count is high, your dog might suffer but don't expect them to sneeze and have runny noses like humans. Dogs react to pollen allergies the same way they react to fleas—they scratch and bite themselves.

Dogs, like humans, can be tested for allergens. Discuss the testing with your veterinary dermatologist.

FOOD PROBLEMS
FOOD ALLERGIES
Dogs are allergic to many foods that are best-sellers and highly recommended by breeders and veterinary surgeons. Changing the brand of food that you buy may not eliminate the problem if the element to which the dog is allergic is contained in the new brand.

Recognising a food allergy is difficult. Humans vomit or have rashes when they eat a food to which they are allergic. Dogs neither vomit nor (usually) develop a rash. They react in the same manner as they do to an airborne or flea allergy: they itch, scratch and bite. Thus making the diagnosis extremely difficult. Whilst pollen allergies and parasite bites are usually seasonal,

POISONOUS PLANTS

Below is a partial list of plants that are considered poisonous. These plants can cause skin irritation, illness, and even death. You should be aware of the types of plants that grow in your garden and that you keep in your home. Special care should be taken to rid your garden of dangerous plants and to keep all plants in the household out of your Shih Tzu's reach.

American Blue Flag	False Acacia	Mistletoe (berries)
Bachelor's Button	Fern	Monkshood
Barberry	Foxglove	Mullein
Bog Iris	Hellebore	Narcissus
Boxwood	Herb of Grace	Peony
Buttercup	Holly	Persian Ivy
Cherry Pits	Horse Chestnut	Rhododendron
Chinese Arbor	Iris (bulb)	Rhubarb
Chokecherry	Japanese Yew	Shallon
Christmas Rose	Jerusalem Cherry	Solomon's Seal
Climbing Lily	Jimson Weed	Star of Bethlehem
Crown of Thorns	Lenten Rose	Water Lily
Elderberry (berries)	Lily of the Valley	Wood Spurge
Elephant Ear	Marigold	Wisteria
English Ivy	Milkwort	Yew

food allergies are year-round problems.

FOOD INTOLERANCE

Food intolerance is the inability of the dog to completely digest certain foods. Puppies that may have done very well on their mother's milk may not do well on cow's milk. The rest of this food intolerance may be evident in the form of loose bowels, passing gas and stomach pains. These are the only obvious symptoms of food intolerance and that makes diagnosis difficult.

TREATING FOOD PROBLEMS

It is possible to handle food allergies and food intolerance yourself. Put your dog on a diet that it has never had. Obviously if it has never eaten this new food it can't have been allergic or intolerant of it. Start with a single ingredient that is not in the dog's diet at the present time. Ingredients like chopped beef or fish are common in dog's diets, so try something more exotic like rabbit, pheasant or even just vegetables. Keep the

---

DID YOU KNOW?
Chances are that you and your dog will have the same allergies. Your allergies are readily recognisable and usually easily treated. Your dog's allergies may be masked.

DID YOU KNOW?
The myth that dogs need extra fat in their diets can be harmful. Should your vet recommend extra fat, use safflower oil instead of animal oils. Safflower oil has been shown to be less likely to cause allergic reactions.

---

dog on this diet (with no additives) for a month. If the symptoms of food allergy or intolerance disappear, chances are your dog has a food allergy.

Don't think that the single ingredient cured the problem. You still must find a suitable diet and ascertain which ingredient in the old diet was objectionable. This is most easily done by adding ingredients to the new diet one at a time. Let the dog stay on the modified diet for a month before you add another ingredient. Eventually, you will determine the ingredient that caused the adverse reaction.

An alternative method is to carefully study the ingredients in the diet to which your dog is allergic or intolerant. Identify the main ingredient in this diet and eliminate the main ingredient by buying a different food that does not have that ingredient. Keep experimenting until the symptoms disappear after one month on the new diet.

A scanning electron micrograph (S. E. M.) of a dog flea, *Ctenocephalides canis.*

S. E. M. BY DR DENNIS KUNKEL, UNIVERSITY OF HAWAII

EXTERNAL PARASITES

Of all the problems to which dogs are prone, none is more well known and frustrating than fleas. Fleas, which usually refers to fleas, ticks and mites, are difficult to prevent but relatively simple to cure. Parasites that are harboured inside the body are more difficult to cure but they are easier to control.

FLEAS

To control a flea infestation you have to understand the life cycle of a typical flea. Fleas are often

thought of as a summertime problem but centrally heated homes have rather changed the pattern and fleas can be found at any time of the year. There is no single flea-control medicine (insecticide) that can be used in every flea-infested area. To understand flea control you must apply suitable treatment to the weak link in the life cycle of the flea.

THE LIFE CYCLE OF A FLEA

Fleas are found in four forms: eggs, larvae, pupae and adults. You really need a low-power microscope or hand lens to identify a living flea's eggs, pupae or

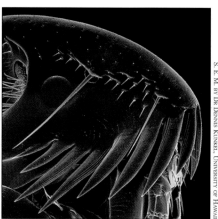

Magnified head of a dog flea, *Ctenocephalides canis.*

S. E. M. BY DR DENNIS KUNKEL, UNIVERSITY OF HAWAII

DID YOU KNOW?

Fleas have been around for millions of years and have adapted to changing host animals.

They are able to go through a complete life cycle in less than one month or they can extend their lives to almost two years by remaining as pupae or cocoons. They do not need blood or any other food for up to 20 months.

They have been measured as being able to jump 300,000 times and can jump 150 times their length in any direction including straight up. Those are just a few of the reasons they are so successful in infesting a dog!

DID YOU KNOW?
Flea-killers are poisonous. You should not spray these toxic chemicals on areas of the dog's body that he licks, on his genitals or on his face. Flea-killers taken internally are a better answer, but check with your vet in case internal therapy is not advised for your dog.

larva. They spend their whole lives on your Shih Tzu unless they are forcibly removed by brushing, bathing, scratching or biting.

The dog flea is scientifically known as *Ctenocephalides canis* whilst the cat flea is *Ctenocephalides felis*. Several species infest both dog and cats.

Fleas lay eggs whilst they are in residence upon your dog.

DID YOU KNOW?
Dogs who have been exposed to lawns sprayed with herbicides have double and triple the rate of malignant lymphoma. Town dogs are especially at risk, as they are exposed to tailored yards and gardens. Dogs perspire and absorb through their footpads. Be careful where your dog walks and always avoid any area that appears yellowed from chemical overspray.

These eggs fall off almost as soon as they dry (they may be a bit damp when initially laid) and are the reservoir of future flea infestations. If your dog scratches himself and is able to dislodge a few fleas, they simply fall off and await a future chance to attack a dog...or even a person. Yes, fleas from dogs bite people. That's why it is so important to control fleas both on the dog and in the dog's entire environment. You must, therefore, treat the dog and the environment simultaneously.

DE-FLEAING THE HOME
Cleanliness is the simple rule. If you have a cat living with your dog, the matter is more complicated

DID YOU KNOW?
There are many parasiticides which can be used around your home and garden to control fleas.

Natural pyrethrins can be used inside the house.

Allethrin, bioallethrin, permethrin and resmethrin can also be used inside the house but permethrin has been used successfully outdoors, too.

Carbaryl can be used indoors and outdoors.

Propoxur can be used indoors.

Chlorpyrifos, diazinon and malathion can be used indoors or outdoors and it has an extended residual activity.

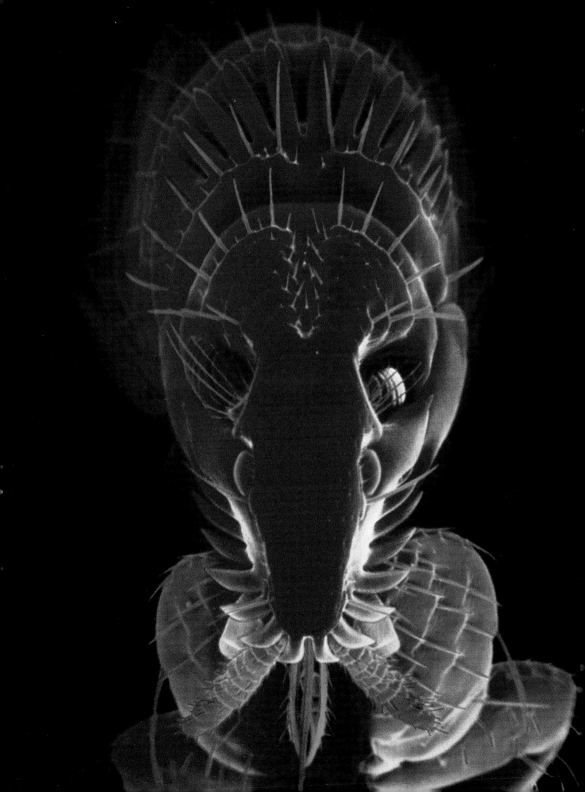

since most dog fleas are actually cat fleas. Cats climb onto many areas that are never accessible to dogs (like window sills, table tops, etc.), so you have to clean all of these areas. The hard floor surfaces (tiles, wood, stone and linoleum) must be mopped several times a day. Drops of food onto the floor are actually food for flea larvae! All rugs and furniture must be vacuumed several times a day. Don't forget cupboards, under furniture and cushions. A study has reported that a vacuum cleaner with a beater bar can remove only 20% of the larvae and 50% of the eggs. The vacuum bags should be discarded into a sealed plastic bag

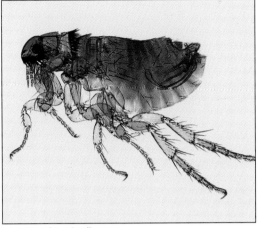

A male dog flea, *Ctenocephalides canis.*

PHOTO BY JEAN CLAUDE REVY/PHOTOTAKE.

DID YOU KNOW?
Never mix flea control products without first consulting your veterinary surgeon. Some products can become toxic when combined with others and can cause serious or fatal consequences.

or burned. The vacuum machine itself should be cleaned. The outdoor area to which your dog has access must also be treated with an insecticide.

Your vet will be able to recommend a household insecticidal spray but this must be used

DID YOU KNOW?
Ivermectin is quickly becoming the drug of choice for treating many parasitic skin diseases in dogs.

For some unknown reason, herding dogs like Collies, Old English Sheepdogs and German Shepherds, etc., are extremely sensitive to ivermectin.

Ivermectin injections have killed some dogs. The ivermectin reaction is a toxicosis which causes tremors, loss of power to move their muscles, prolonged dilatation of the pupil of the eye, coma (unconsciousness), or cessation of breathing (death).

The toxicosis usually starts from 4-6 hours after ingestion or as late as 12 hours. The longer it takes to set in, the milder is the reaction.

Ivermectin should only be prescribed and administered by a vet.

Some ivermectin treatments require two doses.

(Facing Page) A scanning electron micrograph of a dog or cat flea, *Ctenocephalides,* magnified more than 100x. This has been colourised for effect.

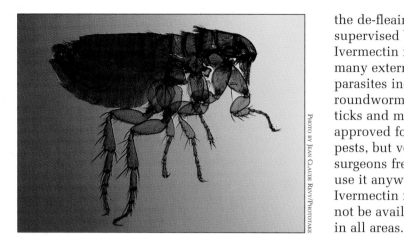

PHOTO BY JEAN CLAUDE REVY/PHOTOTAKE

Male cat fleas, *Ctenocephalides felis*, are very commonly found on dogs.

Dwight R. Kuhn's magnificent action photo showing a flea jumping from a dog's back.

PHOTO BY DWIGHT R KUHN

the de-fleaing and de-worming supervised by your vet. Ivermectin is effective against many external and internal parasites including heartworms, roundworms, tapeworms, flukes, ticks and mites. It has not been approved for use to control these pests, but veterinary surgeons frequently use it anyway. Ivermectin may not be available in all areas.

with caution and instructions strictly adhered to.

There are many drugs available to kill fleas on the dog itself, such as the miracle drug ivermectin, and it is best to have

DID YOU KNOW?

There are drugs which prevent fleas from maturing from egg to adult.

The weak link is the maturation from a larva to a pupa.

Methoprene and fenoxycarb mimic the effect of maturation enhancers, thus, in effect, killing the larva before it pupates.

Methoprene is very effective in killing flea eggs while fenoxycarb is better able to stand UV rays from the sun. There is a combination of both drugs which has an effective life of 6 months and destroys 93% of the flea population.

It is important, in order to effectively control fleas, that you use products designed to kill fleas at all stages of growth, Manufacturers make such products, which are specifically designed for this purpose, and specially made to be safe for use in the home and on the dog.

The Life Cycle of the Flea

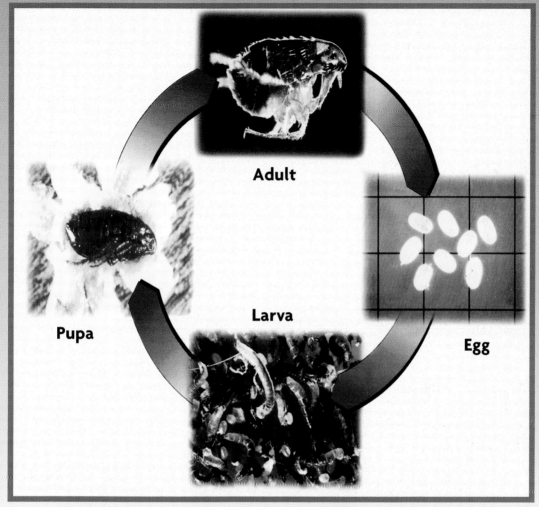

Adult

Pupa

Larva

Egg

The life cycle of the flea was posterised by Fleabusters®. Poster Courtesy of Fleabusters®, R\x for Fleas.

STERILISING THE ENVIRONMENT

Besides cleaning your home with vacuum cleaners and mops, you have to treat the outdoor range of your dog. When trimming bushes and spreading insecticide, be careful not to poison areas in which fishes or other animals reside.

DID YOU KNOW?

Never mix flea control products without first consulting your veterinary surgeon. Some products can become toxic when combined with others and can cause serious or fatal consequences.

TICKS AND MITES

Though not as common as fleas, ticks and mites are found all over the tropical and temperate world. They don't bite like fleas, they harpoon. They dig their sharp proboscis (nose) into the dog's skin and drink the blood, which is their only food and drink. Dogs can get paralysis, Lyme disease, Rocky Mountain spotted fever (normally found in the U.S.A. only), and many other diseases from ticks and mites. They may live where fleas are found but they also like to hide in cracks or seams in walls wherever dogs live. They are controlled the same way fleas are controlled.

The tick *Dermacentor variabilis* may well be the most common dog tick in many geographical areas, especially where the climate is hot and humid.

Most dog ticks have life expectancies of a week to six

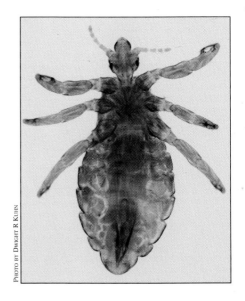

PHOTO BY DWIGHT R KUHN

months, depending upon climatic conditions. They neither jump nor fly, but crawl slowly and can range up to 5 metres (16 feet) to reach a sleeping or unsuspecting dog.

MANGE

Mange is a skin irritation caused by mites. Some mites are contagious, like *Cheyletiella*, ear mites, scabies and chiggers. The non-contagious mites are *Demodex*. The most serious of the mites is the one that causes ear-mite infestation. Ear mites are usually controlled with ivermectin.

It is essential that your dog be treated for mange as quickly as possible because some forms of mange are transmissible to people.

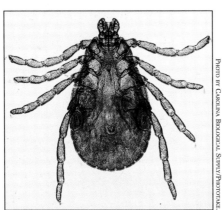

PHOTO BY CAROLINA BIOLOGICAL SUPPLY/PHOTOTAKE.

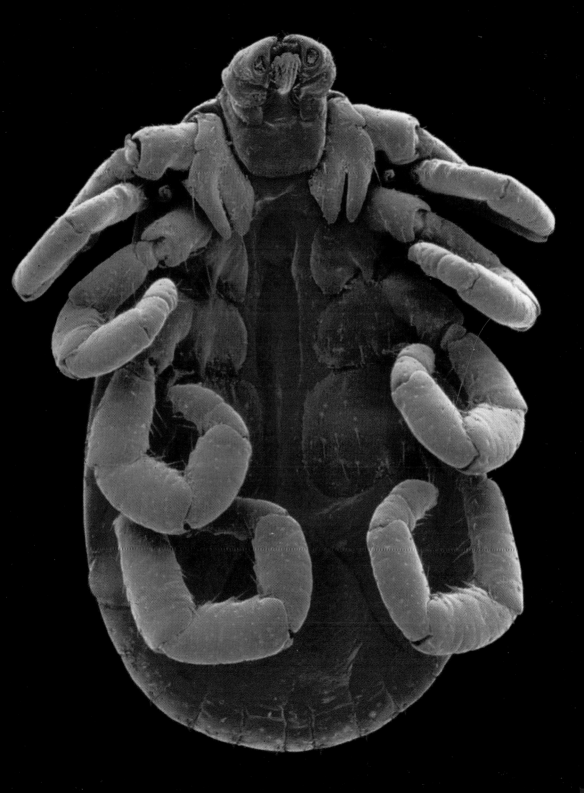

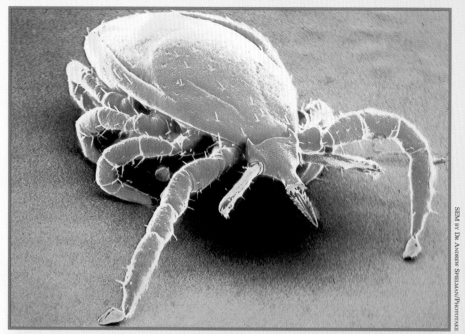

A deer tick, the carrier of Lyme disease.

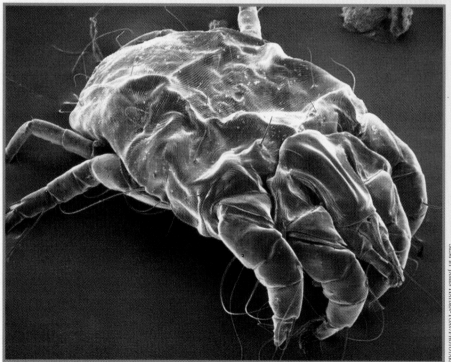

The mange mite, *Psoroptes bovis.*

AUTO-IMMUNE SKIN CONDITIONS

Auto-immune skin conditions are commonly referred to as being allergic to yourself, whilst allergies are usually inflammatory reactions to an outside stimulus. Auto-immune diseases cause serious damage to the tissues that are involved.

The best known auto-immune disease is lupus, which affects people as well as dogs. The symptoms are variable and may affect the kidneys, bones, blood chemistry and skin. It can be fatal to both dogs and humans, though it is not thought to be transmissible. It is usually successfully treated with cortisone, prednisone or similar corticosteroid, but extensive use of these drugs can have harmful side effects.

INTERNAL PARASITES

Most animals—fishes, birds and mammals, including dogs and humans—have worms and other parasites that live inside their bodies. According to Dr Herbert R Axelrod, the fish pathologist, there are two kinds of parasites: dumb and smart. The smart parasites live in peaceful cooperation with their hosts (symbiosis), whilst the dumb parasites kill their host. Most of the worm infections are relatively easy to control. If they are not controlled they eventually weaken the host dog to the point that other medical problems occur, but they are not dumb parasites that directly cause the death of their hosts.

ROUNDWORMS

The roundworms that infect dogs are scientifically known as *Toxocara canis*. They live in the dog's intestine and shed eggs continually. It has been estimated that an average-sized dog produces about 150 grammes of faeces every day. Each gramme of

DID YOU KNOW?

Ridding your puppy of worms is VERY IMPORTANT because certain worms that puppies carry, such as tapeworms and roundworms, can infect humans.

Breeders initiate a deworming programme at or about four weeks of age. The routine is repeated every two or three weeks until the puppy is three months old. The breeder from whom you obtained your puppy should provide you with the complete details of the deworming programme.

Your veterinary surgeon can prescribe and monitor the programme of deworming for you. The usual programme is treating the puppy every 15 to 20 days until the puppy is positively worm free.

It is not advised that you treat your puppy with drugs that are not recommended professionally.

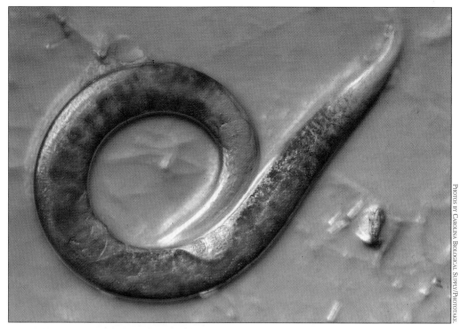

Two views of the roundworm, *Rhabditis*. The roundworm can infect both dogs and humans.

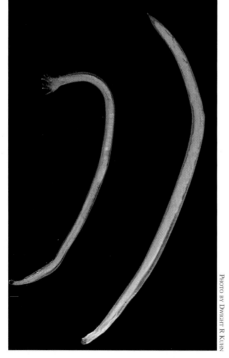

Male and female hookworms, *Ancylostoma caninum*, are uncommonly found in pet or show dogs in Britain. Hookworms may infect other dogs that have exposure to grasslands.

faeces averages 10,000–12,000 eggs of roundworms. All areas in which dogs roam contain astronomical numbers of roundworm eggs. The greatest danger of roundworms is that they infect people, too! It is wise to have your dog tested regularly for roundworms.

Pigs also have roundworm infections that can be passed to human and dogs. The typical pig roundworm parasite is called *Ascaris lumbricoides*.

HOOKWORMS

The worm *Ancylostoma caninum* is commonly called the dog hookworm. It is also dangerous to humans and cats. It attaches itself to the dog's intestines by its teeth. It changes the site of its attachment about six times a day, and the dog loses blood from each detachment. This blood loss can cause iron-deficiency anaemia. Hookworms are easily purged from the dog with many medications, the best of which seems to be ivermectin even though it has not been approved for such use.

In Britain, the 'temperate climate' hookworm (*Uncinaria stenocephala*) is rarely found in pet or show dogs, but can occur in hunting packs, racing Greyhounds and sheepdogs because these hookworms can be prevalent wherever dogs are exercised regularly on grassland.

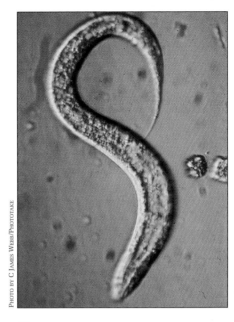

PHOTO BY C. JAMES WEBB/PHOTOTAKE

The infective stage of the hookworm larva.

ROUNDWORMS

Average size dogs can pass 1,360,000 roundworm eggs every day.

For example, if there were only 1 million dogs in the world, the world would be saturated with 1,300 metric tonnes of dog faeces. These faeces would contain 15,000,000,000 roundworm eggs.

7 to 31 percent of home gardens and children's play boxes in the U. S. contained roundworm eggs.

Flushing dog's faeces down the toilet is not a safe practice because the usual sewage treatments do not destroy roundworm eggs.

Infected puppies start shedding roundworm eggs at 3 weeks of age. They can be infected by their mother's milk.

TAPEWORMS

There are many species of tapeworms, many of which are carried by fleas! The dog eats the flea and starts the tapeworm cycle. Humans can also be infected with tapeworms, so don't eat fleas! Fleas are so small that your dog could pass them onto your hands, your plate or your food and make it possible for you to ingest a flea which is carrying tapeworm eggs.

Whilst tapeworm infection is not life threatening in dogs (smart parasite!), it can be the cause of a very serious liver disease for humans. About 50 percent of the humans infected with *Echinococcus multilocularis*, causing alveolar hydatis, perish.

TAPEWORMS

Humans, rats, squirrels, foxes, coyotes, wolves, mixed breeds of dogs and purebred dogs are all susceptible to tapeworm infection. Except in humans, tapeworms are usually not a fatal infection. Infected individuals can harbour a thousand parasitic worms. Tapeworms have two sexes—male and female (many other worms have only one sex—male and female in the same worm). If dogs eat infected rats or mice, they get the tapeworm disease.

One month after attaching to a dog's intestine, the worm starts shedding eggs. These eggs are infective immediately. Infective eggs can live for a few months without a host animal. Roundworms, whipworms and tapeworms are just a few of the other commonly known worms that infect dogs.

The head and rostellum (the round prominence on the scolex) of a tapeworm, which infects dogs and humans.

HEARTWORMS

Heartworms are thin, extended worms up to 30 cms. (12 ins.) long that live in a dog's heart and the major blood vessels around it. Shih Tzu may have up to 200 of these worms. The symptoms may be loss of energy, loss of appetite, coughing, the development of a pot belly and anaemia.

Heartworms are transmitted by mosquitoes. The mosquito drinks the blood of an infected dog and takes in larvae with the blood. The larvae, called microfilaria, develop within the body of the mosquito and are passed on to the next dog bitten after the larvae mature. It takes two to three weeks for the larvae to develop to the infective stage within the body of the mosquito. Dogs should be treated at about six weeks of age, then every six months.

Blood testing for heartworms is not necessarily indicative of how seriously your dog is infected. This is a dangerous disease. Although heartworm affects dogs in America, Asia, Australia, and Central Europe, dogs in Britain are not affected by heartworm.

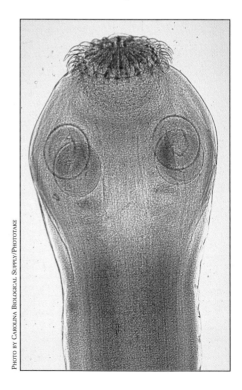

PHOTO BY CAROLINA BIOLOGICAL SUPPLY/PHOTOTAKE

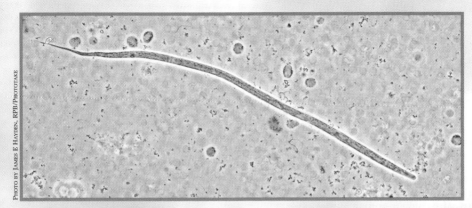

The heartworm, *Dirofilaria immitis.*

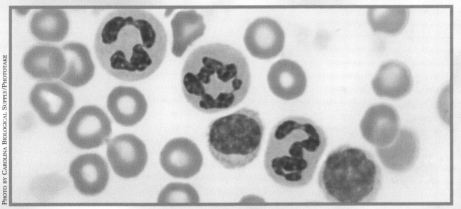

Magnified heartworm larvae, *Dirofilaria immitis.*

The heart of a dog infected with canine heartworm, *Dirofilaria immitis.*

CDS: COGNITIVE DYSFUNCTION SYNDROME
"Old Dog Syndrome"

There are many ways to evaluate old-dog syndrome. Veterinary surgeons have defined CDS (cognitive dysfunction syndrome) as the gradual deterioration of cognitive abilities. These are indicated by changes in the dog's behaviour. When a dog changes its routine response, and maladies have been eliminated as the cause of these behavioural changes, then CDS is the usual diagnosis.

More than half the dogs over 8 years old suffer some form of CDS. The older the dog, the more chance it has of suffering from CDS. In humans, doctors often dismiss the CDS behavioural changes as part of 'winding down.'

There are four major signs of CDS: frequent toilet accidents inside the home, sleeps much more or much less than normal, acts confused, and fails to respond to social stimuli.

SYMPTOMS OF CDS

FREQUENT TOILET ACCIDENTS
- *Urinates in the house.*
- *Defecates in the house.*
- *Doesn't signal that he wants to go out.*

SLEEP PATTERNS
- *Moves much more slowly.*
- *Sleeps more than normal during the day.*
- *Sleeps less during the night.*
- *Walks around listlessly and without a destination goal.*

CONFUSION
- *Goes outside and just stands there.*
- *Appears confused with a faraway look in his eyes.*
- *Hides more often.*
- *Doesn't recognise friends.*
- *Doesn't come when called.*

FAILS TO RESPOND TO SOCIAL STIMULI
- *Comes to people less frequently, whether called or not.*
- *Doesn't tolerate petting for more than a short time.*
- *Doesn't come to the door when you return home from work.*

YOUR SENIOR
Shih Tzu

The term old is a qualitative term. For dogs, as well as their masters, old is relative. Certainly we can all distinguish between a puppy Shih Tzu and an adult Shih Tzu—there are the obvious physical traits, such as size, appearance and facial expressions, and personality traits. Puppies that are nasty are very rare. Puppies and young dogs like to play with children. Children's natural exuberance is a good match for the seemingly endless energy of young dogs. They like to run, jump, chase and retrieve. When dogs grow up and cease their interaction with children, they are often thought of as being too old to play with the kids.

On the other hand, if a Shih Tzu is only exposed to people over 60 years of age, its life will normally be less active and it will not seem to be getting old as its activity level slows down.

If people live to be 100 years old, dogs live to be 20 years old. Whilst this is a good rule of thumb, it is very inaccurate. When trying to compare dog years to human years, you cannot make a generalisation about all dogs. You can make the generalisation

that, 15 years is a good life span for a Shih Tzu, which is quite good compared to many other purebred dogs that may only live to 8 or 9 years of age. Some Shih Tzu have been known to live to 20 years. Dogs are generally considered mature within three years, but they can reproduce even earlier. So the first three years of a dog's life are like seven times that of comparable humans. That means a 3-year-old dog is like a 21-year-old human. As the curve of comparison shows, there is no hard and fast rule for comparing dog and human ages. The comparison is made even

> **DID YOU KNOW?**
> The bottom line is simply that a dog is getting old when YOU think it is getting old because it slows down in its general activities, including walking, running, eating, jumping and retrieving. On the other hand, certain activities increase, like more sleeping, more barking and more repetition of habits like going to the door when you put your coat on without being called.

more difficult, for not all humans age at the same rate...and human females live longer than human males.

WHAT TO LOOK FOR IN SENIORS

Most veterinary surgeons and behaviourists use the seventh year mark as the time to consider a dog a 'senior.' The term 'senior' does not imply that the dog is geriatric and has begun to fail in mind and body. Ageing is essentially a slowing process. Humans readily admit that they feel a difference in their activity level from age 20 to 30, and then from 30 to 40, etc. By treating the seven-year-old dog

as a senior, owners are able to implement certain therapeutic and preventive medical strategies with the help of their veterinary surgeons. A senior-care programme should include at least two veterinary visits per year, screening sessions to determine the dog's health status, as well as nutritional counselling. Veterinary surgeons determine the senior dog's health status through a blood smear for a complete blood count, serum chemistry profile with electrolytes, urinalysis, blood pressure check, electrocardiogram, ocular tonometry (pressure on the eyeball), and dental prophylaxis.

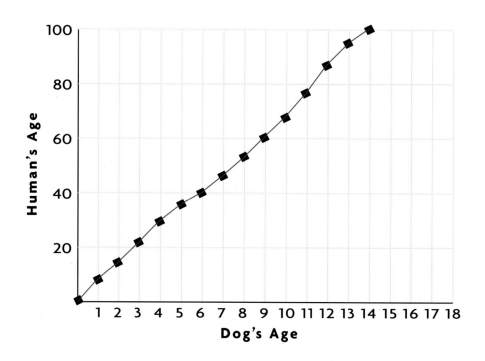

Introducing a second dog into the household with an older Shih Tzu can give the senior newfound energies and motivations. Owners must be sure to lavish equal attention on both dogs.

Such an extensive programme for senior dogs is well advised before owners start to see the obvious physical signs of ageing, such as slower and inhibited movement, greying, increased sleep/nap periods, and disinterest in play and other activity. This preventative programme promises a longer, healthier life for the ageing dog. Amongst the physical problems common in ageing dogs are the loss of sight and vision, arthritis, kidney and liver failure, diabetes mellitus, heart disease, and Cushing's disease (a hormonal disease).

In addition to the physical manifestations discussed, there are some behavioural changes and

DID YOU KNOW?
An old dog starts to show one or more of the following symptoms:

• The hair on its face and paws starts to turn grey. The colour breakdown usually starts around the eyes and mouth.

• Sleep patterns are deeper and longer and the old dog is harder to awaken.

• Food intake diminishes.

• Responses to calls, whistles and other signals are ignored more and more.

• Eye contacts do not evoke tail wagging (assuming they once did).

problems related to ageing dogs. Dogs suffering from hearing or vision loss, dental discomfort or arthritis can become aggressive. Likewise the near-deaf and/or blind dog may be startled more easily and react in an unexpectedly aggressive manner. Seniors suffering from senility can become more impatient and irritable. Housesoiling accidents are associated with loss of mobility, kidney problems, loss of sphincter control as well as plaque accumulation, physiological brain changes, and reactions to medications. Older dogs, just like young puppies, suffer from separation anxiety, which can lead to excessive barking, whining, housesoiling, and destructive behaviour. Seniors may become fearful of everyday sounds, such as vacuum cleaners, heaters, thunder, and passing traffic. Some dogs have difficulty sleeping, due to discomfort, the need for frequent potty visits, and the like. Owners should avoid spoiling the older dog with too many fatty treats. Obesity is a common problem in older dogs and subtracts years from their lifespan. Keep the senior dog as trim as possible since excessive weight puts additional stress on the body's vital organs. Some breeders recommend supplementing the diet with foods high in fibre and lower in calories. Adding fresh vegetables and marrow broth to the senior's diet makes a tasty, low-calorie, low-fat supplement. Vets also offer specialty diets for senior dogs that are worth exploring.

Your dog, as he nears his twilight years, needs his owner's patience and good care more than ever. Never punish an older dog for an accident or abnormal behaviour. For all the years of love, protection and companionship that your dog has provided, he deserves special attention and courtesies. The older dog may

---

DID YOU KNOW?

The symptoms listed below are symptoms that gradually appear and become more noticeable. They are not life threatening, however, the symptoms below are to be taken very seriously and a discussion with your veterinary surgeon is warranted:

• Your dog cries and whimpers when it moves and stops running completely.

• Convulsions start or become more serious and frequent. The usual convulsion (spasm) is when the dog stiffens and starts to tremble being unable or unwilling to move. The seizure usually lasts for 5 to 30 minutes.

• Your dog drinks more water and urinates more frequently. Wetting and bowel accidents take place indoors without warning.

• Vomiting becomes more and more frequent.

The Shih Tzu owner must take care that his senior dog has appropriate veterinary attention. To ensure your dog's livelihood, twice-annual checkups are advised.

very obvious that you love your Shih Tzu or you would not be reading this book. Putting a loved dog to sleep is extremely difficult. It is a decision that must be made with your veterinary surgeon. You are usually forced to make the decision when one of the life-threatening symptoms listed above becomes serious enough for you to seek medical (veterinary) help.

If the prognosis of the malady indicates the end is near and your beloved pet will only suffer more and experience no enjoyment for the balance of its life, then euthanasia is the right choice.

need to relieve himself at 3 a.m. because he can no longer hold it for eight hours. Older dogs may not be able to remain crated for more than two or three hours. It may be time to give up a sofa or chair to your old friend. Although he may not seem as enthusiastic about your attention and petting, he does appreciate the considerations you offer as he gets older.

Your Shih Tzu does not understand why his world is slowing down. Owners must make the transition into the golden years as pleasant and rewarding as possible.

WHAT TO DO
WHEN THE TIME COMES
You are never fully prepared to make a rational decision about putting your dog to sleep. It is

WHAT IS EUTHANASIA?
Euthanasia derives from the Greek meaning good death. In other words, it means the planned,

DID YOU KNOW?

Fear in an older dog is often the result of improper or incomplete socialisation as a pup, or it can be the result of a traumatic experience he suffered when young. Keep in mind that the term 'traumatic' is relative—something that you would not think twice about can leave a lasting negative impression on a puppy. If the dog experiences a similar experience later in life, he may try to fight back to protect himself. Again, this behaviour is very unpredictable, especially if you do not know what is triggering his fear.

painless killing of a dog suffering from a painful, incurable condition, or who is so aged that it cannot walk, see, eat or control its excretory functions.

Euthanasia is usually accomplished by injection with an overdose of an anaesthesia or barbiturate. Aside from the prick of the needle, the experience is usually painless.

HOW ABOUT YOU?

The decision to euthanize your dog is never easy. The days during which the dog becomes ill and the end occurs can be unusually stressful for you. If this is your first experience with the death of a loved one, you may need the comfort dictated by your religious beliefs. If you are the head of the family and have children, you should have involved them in the decision of putting your Shih Tzu to sleep. Usually your dog can be maintained on drugs for a few days in order to give you ample time to make a decision. During this time, talking with members of your family or even people who have lived through this same experience can ease the burden of your inevitable decision.

THE FINAL RESTING PLACE

Dogs can have some of the same privileges as humans. They can occasionally be buried in their entirety in a pet cemetery which is generally expensive, or if they have died at home can buried in your garden in a place suitably marked with some stone or newly planted tree or bush. Alternatively they can be cremated and the ashes returned to you, or some people prefer to leave their dogs at the surgery for the vet to dispose of.

All of these options should be discussed frankly and openly with your veterinary surgeon. Do not be afraid to ask financial questions. Cremations can be individual, but a less expensive option is mass cremation, although of course the ashes can not then be returned. Vets can usually arrange cremation services on your behalf, but you

DID YOU KNOW?
Euthanasia must be done by a licensed veterinary surgeon. There also may be societies for the prevention of cruelty to animals in your area. They often offer this service upon a vet's recommendation.

must be aware that in Britain if your dog has died at the surgery the vet cannot legally allow you to take your dog's body home.

GETTING ANOTHER DOG?

The grief of losing your beloved dog will be as lasting as the grief of losing a human friend or relative. You cannot go out and buy another grandfather, but you can go out and buy another Shih Tzu. In most cases, if your dog died of old age (if there is such a thing), it had slowed down considerably. Do you want a new Shih Tzu puppy to replace it? Or are you better off in finding a more mature Shih Tzu, say two to three years of age, which will usually be housetrained and will have an already developed personality. In this case, you can find out if you like each other after a few hours of being together.

Many pet cemeteries have facilities for storing a dog's ashes.

The decision is, of course, your own. Do you want another Shih Tzu or perhaps a different breed so as to avoid comparison with your beloved friend? Most people usually buy the same breed because they know (and love) the characteristics of that breed. Then, too, they often know people who have the same breed and perhaps they are lucky enough that a breeder they know and respect expects a litter soon. What could be better?

Consult your veterinary surgeon to help you locate a pet cemetery in your area.

SHOWING YOUR
Shih Tzu

When you purchased your Shih Tzu you will have made it clear to the breeder whether you wanted one just as a loveable companion and pet, or if you hoped to be buying a Shih Tzu with show prospects. No reputable breeder will have sold you a young puppy puppy with 'show potential'.

To the novice, exhibiting a Shih Tzu in the show ring may look easy but it usually takes a lot of hard work and devotion to do top winning at a show such as the prestigious Crufts, not to mention a little luck too!

Few breeds are the natural show dogs that Shih Tzu are! The proud owners love to give their dogs the opportunity to show off a bit.

saying that it was definitely of show quality for so much can go wrong during the early weeks and months of a puppy's development. If you plan to show, what you will hopefully have acquired is a

The first concept that the canine novice learns when watching a dog show is that each breed first competes against members of its own breed. Once the judge has selected the best member of each breed, provided that the show is judged on a Group system, that chosen dog will compete with other dogs in its group. Finally the best of each group will compete for Best in Show and Reserve Best in Show.

The second concept that you must understand is that the dogs are not actually competing against one another. The judge compares

SHOW DIVISIONS
The Kennel Club divides its dogs into seven Groups: Gundogs, Utility, Working, Toy, Terrier, Hounds and Pastoral.*

*The Pastoral Group, established in 1999, includes those sheepdog breeds previously categorised in the Working Group.

A junior winning bitch at a local club show. The author awarded this lovely bitch a ticket at a breed show.

each dog against the breed standard, which is a written description of the ideal specimen of the breed. Whilst some early breed standards were indeed based on specific dogs that were famous or popular, many dedicated enthusiasts say that a perfect specimen, described in the standard, has never been bred. Thus the 'perfect' dog never walked into a show ring, has never been bred and, to the woe of dog breeders around the globe, does not exist. Breeders attempt to get as close to this ideal as possible, with every litter, but theoretically the 'perfect' dog is so elusive that it is impossible. (And if the 'perfect' dog were born, breeders and judges would never agree that it was indeed 'perfect.')

If you are interested in exploring dog shows, your best bet is to join your local breed club. These clubs often host both Championship and Open shows, and

WINNING THE TICKET
Earning a championship at Kennel Club shows is the most difficult in the world. Compared to the United States and Canada where it is relatively not 'challenging,' collecting three green tickets not only requires much time and effort, it can be very expensive! Challenge Certificates, as the tickets are properly known, are the building blocks of champions—good breeding, good handling, good training and good luck!

sometimes Match meetings and Special Events, all of which could be of interest, even if you are only an onlooker. Clubs also send out newsletters and some organise training days and seminars in order that people may learn more about their chosen breed. To locate the nearest breed club for you, contact The Kennel Club, the ruling body for the British dog world. The Kennel Club governs not only conformation shows but also

DID YOU KNOW?

Just like with anything else, there is a certain etiquette to the show ring that can only be learned through experience. Showing your dog can be quite intimidating to you as a novice when it seems as if everyone else knows what he's doing. You can familiarise yourself with ring procedure beforehand by taking a class to prepare you and your dog for conformation showing or by talking with an experienced handler. When you are in the ring, listen and pay attention to the judge and follow his/her directions. Remember, even the most skilled handlers had to start somewhere. Keep it up and you too will become a proficient handler before too long!

working trials, obedience trials, agility trials and field trials. The Kennel Club furnishes the rules and regulations for all these events plus general dog registration and other basic requirements of dog ownership. Its annual show called the Crufts Dogs Show, held in Birmingham, is the largest bench show in England. Every year over 20,000 of the U.K.'s best dogs qualify to participate in this marvellous show which lasts four days.

The Kennel Club governs many different kinds of shows in Great Britain, Australia, South Africa and beyond. At the most competitive and prestigious of these shows, the Championship Shows, a dog can earn Challenge Certificates, and thereby become a Show Champion or a Champion. A dog must earn three Challenge Certificates under three different judges to earn the prefix of 'Sh Ch' or 'Ch' Note that some breeds must also qualify in a field trial in order to gain the title of full champion. Challenge Certificates are awarded to a very small percentage of the dogs competing, especially as dogs which are already Champions compete with others for these coveted CCs. The number of Challenge Certificates awarded in any one year is based upon the total number of dogs in each breed entered for competition. There three types of Championship Shows, an all-

Breeders and owners take great pride in their winning dogs. This flawless show dog has a handsome silver cup to sleep in tonight!

breed General Championship Show for all Kennel Club recognised breeds, a Group Championship Show, limited to breeds within one of the groups, and a Breed Show, usually confined to a single breed. The Kennel Club determines which breeds at which Championship Shows will have the opportunity to earn Challenge Certificates (or tickets). Serious exhibitors often will opt not to participate if the tickets are withheld at a particular show. This policy makes earning championships ever more difficult to accomplish.

Open Shows are generally less competitive and are frequently used as 'practice shows' for young dogs. There are hundreds of Open Shows each year that can be

CLASSES AT DOG SHOWS

There can be as many as 18 classes per sex for your breed. Check the show schedule carefully to make sure that you have entered your dog in the appropriate class. Among the classes offered can be: Beginners; Minor Puppy (ages 6 to 9 months); Puppy (ages 6 to 12 months); Junior (ages 6 to 18 months); Beginners (handler or dog never won first place) as well as the following, each of which is defined in the schedule: Maiden; Novice; Tyro; Debutant; Undergraduate; Graduate; Postgraduate; Minor Limit; Mid Limit; Limit; Open; Veteran; Stud Dog; Brood Bitch; Progeny; Brace and Team.

Grooming the Shih Tzu to have correct expression and balance requires skill and experience. When groomed properly, the Shih Tzu possesses a dignity and wisdom that is ineffable.

invitingly social events and are great first show experiences for the novice. Even if you're considering just watching a show to wet your paws, an Open Show is a great choice.

Whilst Championship and Open Shows are most important for the beginner to understand, there are other types of shows in which the interested dog owner can participate. Training clubs sponsor Matches that can be entered on the day of the show for a nominal fee. In these introductory-level exhibitions, two dogs are pulled out of a hat and 'matched,' the winner of that match goes on to the next round, and eventually only one dog is left undefeated.

Exemption Shows are much more light-hearted affairs with usually only four pedigree

classes and several 'fun' classes, all of which can be entered on the day. The proceeds of an Exemption Show must be given to a charity and are sometimes held in conjunction with small agricultural shows. Limited Shows are also available in small number, but entry is restricted to members of the club which hosts the show, although one can usually join the club when making an entry.

Before you actually step into the ring, you would be well advised to sit back and observe the judge's ring procedure. If it is your first time in the ring, do not be over-anxious and run to the front of the line. It is much better to stand back and study how the exhibitor in front of you

HOW TO ENTER A DOG SHOW

1. Obtain an entry form and show schedule from the Show Secretary.
2. Select the classes that you want to enter and complete the entry form.
3. Transfer your dog into your name at The Kennel Club. (Be sure that this matter is handled before entering.)
4. Find out how far in advance show entries must be made. Oftentimes it's more than a couple of months.

Your winning entry could garner a ribbon, a trophy, or a medal, depending on the venue and the type of contest.

is performing. The judge asks each handler to 'stand' the dog, hopefully showing the dog off to his best advantage. The judge will observe the dog from a distance and from different angles, approach the dog, check his teeth, overall structure, alertness and muscle tone, as well as consider how well the dog 'conforms' to the standard. Most importantly, the judge will have the exhibitor move the dog around the ring in some pattern that he or she should specify (another advantage to not going first, but always listen since some judges change their directions, and the judge is always right!) Finally the judge will give the dog one last look before moving on to the next exhibitor.

If you are not in the top three at your first show, do not be discouraged. Be patient and consistent and you may eventually find yourself in the winning lineup. Remember that the winners were once in your shoes and have devoted many hours and much money to earn the placement. If you find that your dog is losing every time and never getting a nod, it may be time to consider a different dog sport or just enjoy your Shih Tzu as a pet.

WORKING TRIALS
Working trials can be entered by any well-trained dog of any breed, not just Gundogs or Working dogs. Many dogs that earn the Kennel Club Good Citizen Dog award choose to participate in a working

The dog walk is a common obstacle in agility trials.

trial. There are five stakes at both open and championship levels: Companion Dog (CD), Utility Dog (UD), Working Dog (WD), Tracking Dog (TD), and Patrol Dog (PD). As in conformation shows, dogs compete against a standard and if the dog reaches the qualifying mark, it obtains a certificate. Divided into groups, each exercise must be achieved 70 percent in order to qualify. If the dog achieves 80 percent in the open level, it receives a Certificate of Merit (COM), in the championship level, it receives a Qualifying Certificate. At the CD stake, dogs must participate in

four groups, Control, Stay, Agility and Search (Retrieve and Nosework). At the next three levels, UD, WD and TD, there are only three groups: Control, Agility and Nosework.

Agility consists of three jumps: a vertical scale up a six-foot wall of planks; a clear jump over a basic three-foot hurdle with a removable top bar; and a long jump across angled planks stretching nine feet.

To earn the UD, WD and TD, dogs must track approximately one-half mile for articles laid from one-half hour to three hours ago. Tracks consist of turns and legs, and fresh ground is used for each participant.

The fifth stake, PD, involves teaching manwork, which is not recommended for every breed.

FIELD TRIALS AND WORKING TESTS
Working tests are frequently used to prepare dogs for field trials, the purpose of which is to heighten the instincts and natural abilities of gundogs. Live game is

---

DID YOU KNOW?

You can get information about dog shows from kennel clubs and breed clubs:

Fédération Cynologique Internationale
14, rue Leopold II, B-6530 Thuin, Belgium
www.fci.be

The Kennel Club
1-5 Clarges St., Piccadilly, London
W1Y 8AB, UK
www.the-kennel-club.org.uk

American Kennel Club
5580 Centerview Dr., Raleigh, NC
27606-3390, USA
www.akc.org

Canadian Kennel Club
89 Skyway Ave., Suite 100, Etobicoke,
Ontario M9W 6R4 Canada
www.ckc.ca

not used in working tests. Unlike field trials, working tests do not count toward a dog's record at The Kennel Club, though the same judges often oversee working tests. Field trials began in England in 1947 and are only moderately popular amongst dog folk. Whilst breeders of Working and Gundog breeds concern themselves with the field abilities of their dogs, there is considerably less interest in field trials than dog shows. In order for dogs to become full champions, certain breeds must qualify in the field as well. Upon gaining three CCs in the show ring, the dog is designated a Show Champion (Sh Ch). The title Champion (Ch) requires that the dog gain an award at a field trial, be a 'special qualifier' at a field trial or pass a 'special show dog qualifier' judged by a field trial judge on a shooting day.

At agility trials, the Shih Tzu is motivated, agile and success-oriented! This contestant is on the teeter-totter.

course that includes jumps (such as those used in the working trials), as well as tyres, the dog walk, weave poles, pipe tunnels, collapsed tunnels, etc. The Kennel Club requires that dogs not be trained for agility until they are 12 months old. This dog sport intends to be great fun for dog and owner and interested owners should join a training club that has obstacles and experienced agility handlers who can introduce you and your dog to the 'ropes' (and tyres, tunnels and so on).

AGILITY TRIALS

Agility trials began in the United Kingdom in 1977 and have since spread around the world, especially to the United States, where it enjoys strong popularity. The handler directs his dog over an obstacle

Pipe tunnels and collapsed tunnels pose no challenge to the trained Shih Tzu.

The world's oldest dog show is the Westminster Kennel Club Dog Show, which takes place annually in New York City. The group finales are completely televised, and the show has an attendance of more than 50,000 people per day.

Now you can understand why the words *Shih Tzu* in Chinese can be translated into *lion's mane*. This 'lion' is proudly enthroned on his perch.

FÉDÉRATION CYNOLOGIQUE INTERNATIONALE

Established in 1911, the Fédération Cynologique Internationale (FCI) represents the 'world kennel club.' This international body brings uniformity to the breeding, judging and showing of purebred dogs. Although the FCI originally included only four European nations: France, Holland, Austria and Belgium (which remains its headquarters), the organisation today embraces nations on six continents and recognises well over 300 breeds of purebred dog. There are three titles attainable through the FCI: the International Champion, which is the most prestigious; the International Beauty Champion, which is based on aptitude certificates in different countries; and the International Trial Champion, which is based on achievement in obedience trials in different countries. Quarantine laws in England and Australia prohibit most of their exhibitors from entering FCI shows. The rest of the Continent does participate in these impressive canine spectacles, the largest of which is the World Dog Show, hosted in a different country each year. FCI sponsors both national and international shows. The hosting country determines the judging system and breed standards are always based on the breed's country of origin.

(FACING PAGE) Groomed meticulously, the American Shih Tzu has quite a different appearance to the British-bred dog. Both the American and British dogs compete at FCI dog shows.

INDEX

Page numbers in **boldface** indicate illustrations.

My Shih Tzu

PUT YOUR PUPPY'S FIRST PICTURE HERE

Dog's Name _____

Date _____ Photographer _____